D0327283

APR 2009

| DATE DUE | | | |
|---|---|---|---|
| | | | |
| | | | |
| | | | |
| | | | |
| | | | |
| | | | |
| | | | |
| | | | |
| | | | |
| | | | |
| | | | |
| | | | |

Farmers Branch Manske Library
13613 Webb Chapel
Farmers Branch, TX 75234-3756

Dondi brings special insights as a business leader with executive level responsibilities. She has a unique ability to dynamically connect the demands of the workplace with the companion demands of family and community. She can open insights that enable discovery of your human potential while simultaneously providing a door toward greater professional effectiveness. Dondi seems to be on a perpetual quest for knowledge that enables discovery of the deeper meaning of nearly all things while you journey with her.

—ERIC GREENWOOD
EXECUTIVE VICE PRESIDENT, RETIRED
BANK OF AMERICA

I am delighted to highly recommend the latest book written by the internationally acclaimed Dondi Scumaci, titled *Ready, Set...Grow!* For those looking for springs of living water to refresh their hearts and lives...read this book!

—JOHN HAGEE
SENIOR PASTOR, CORNERSTONE CHURCH
SAN ANTONIO, TX

I wish I had been exposed to this book at the beginning of my military experience and professional career, before important relationships were formed, rather than near the end of my personal career. Not only does it illuminate the need for hope in our lives and the lives of others with whom we meet on a daily basis, but it is also a road map for proper conduct, respect for personal space, and positive thinking and actions. This information results in growth not only in the business world but also in personal development. I have found many "pearls of wisdom" shared within the confines of this book.

—JACK D. DOWNING
VICE PRESIDENT INTERNATIONAL
CHALLENGER MINERALS INC.

An inspirational book that captures both the best and the worst aspects of our humanity, this book moved me in many ways and reminded me that with hope and faith in God, the undefeatable human spirit can prevail. *Ready, Set...Grow!* is an extraordinary example of Dondi's authorship and insight into what it means to embrace life in the darkest of times.

—VAN MABEE
ANITA GOUDEAU DESIGNS, OWNER

Regardless of your occupation or preoccupation, Dondi Scumaci's *Ready, Set…Grow!* is a loving encouragement for all to take heart, take action, and continue to dream.

—SYBEL M. PICI
OWNER/OPERATOR
PICICO DBA MCDONALD'S RESTAURANTS

Dondi's message can be put into practice immediately in your life to see hope grow, regardless of your situation. It is so much more than just a feel-good message; in a world where hope is being lost and replaced by other things, this is a can-do attitude with doable application.

—KIMBERLY WRAY
HUMAN RESOURCES DIRECTOR
CLEAR CHANNEL COMMUNICATIONS

*Ready, Set…Grow!* is more like a heart-to-heart chat than just a book. Dondi Scumaci breathes the fresh air of hope into our dreams. In this book packed with poignant stories and biblical truths, she gives us practical tools to harness the power of our beliefs. This is a dynamic resource for anyone of any age who hasn't yet reached their goals in life or business.

—CAROL KURTZ
TITLETRAKK.COM

# READY, SET... GROW!

Farmers Branch Manske Library
13613 Webb Chapel
Farmers Branch, TX 75234-3756

## DONDI SCUMACI

**EXcel**
BOOKS
A STRANG COMPANY

Most Strang Communications/Charisma House/Christian Life/ Excel Books/ FrontLine/Realms/Siloam products are available at special quantity discounts for bulk purchase for sales promotions, premiums, fund-raising, and educational needs. For details, write Strang Communications Book Group, 600 Rinehart Road, Lake Mary, Florida 32746, or telephone (407) 333-0600.

Ready, Set…Grow! by Dondi Scumaci
Published by Excel Books
A Strang Company
600 Rinehart Road
Lake Mary, Florida 32746
www.strangdirect.com

This book or parts thereof may not be reproduced in any form, stored in a retrieval system, or transmitted in any form by any means—electronic, mechanical, photocopy, recording, or otherwise—without prior written permission of the publisher, except as provided by United States of America copyright law.

Unless otherwise noted, all Scripture quotations are from the Holy Bible, New Living Translation, copyright © 1996, 2004. Used by permission of Tyndale House Publishers, Inc., Wheaton, IL 60189. All rights reserved.

Scripture quotations marked AMP are from the Amplified Bible. Old Testament copyright © 1965, 1987 by the Zondervan Corporation. The Amplified New Testament copyright © 1954, 1958, 1987 by the Lockman Foundation. Used by permission.

Scripture quotations marked KJV are from the King James Version of the Bible.

Scripture quotations marked NAS are from the New American Standard Bible. Copyright © 1960, 1962, 1963, 1968, 1971, 1972, 1973, 1975, 1977 by the Lockman Foundation. Used by permission. (www.Lockman.org)

Scripture quotations marked NIV are from the Holy Bible, New International Version. Copyright © 1973, 1978, 1984, International Bible Society. Used by permission.

Scripture quotations marked NKJV are from the New King James Version of the Bible. Copyright © 1979, 1980, 1982 by Thomas Nelson, Inc., publishers. Used by permission.

Scripture quotations marked THE MESSAGE are from *The Message: The Bible in Contemporary English*, copyright © 1993, 1994, 1995, 1996, 2000, 2001, 2002. Used by permission of NavPress Publishing Group.

People and incidents in this book are composites created by the author from her experiences in speaking and consulting. Names and details of the stories have been changed, and any similarity between the names and stories of individuals described in this book to individuals known to readers is purely coincidental.

Design Director: Bill Johnson
Cover design by Amanda Potter

Copyright © 2009 by Dondi Scumaci
All rights reserved

Library of Congress Cataloging-in-Publication Data:
Scumaci, Dondi.
  Ready, set-- grow! / Dondi Scumaci. -- 1st ed.
    p. cm.
  Includes bibliographical references (p.     ).
  ISBN 978-1-59979-466-2
  1. Christian women--Religious life. 2. Success--Religious aspects--Christianity. I. Title.
  BV4527.S29 2009
  248.8'43--dc22

                                    2008050073

First Edition

09 10 11 12 13 — 987654321
Printed in the United States of America

## This book is dedicated to those who are searching for hope.

It is for the ones who thought hope might never grow, but who still have the courage to plant again.

It is for the ones who plant hope in others and with great joy watch it grow.

> The wilderness and the dry land shall be glad; the desert shall rejoice and blossom like the rose and the autumn crocus.
>
> —ISAIAH 35:1, AMP

# ACKNOWLEDGMENTS

THANK YOU TO EACH person who has graciously shared your story. Some of your stories are included here—I hope I have honored you by telling them well.

Special thanks to my mothers, Elle and Johnny. You have invested yourselves in me and in this project so beautifully. You are tender of heart and gracious of spirit—two of the most beautiful flowers in my garden.

Deepest gratitude to Pastor John and Diana Hagee for all you have done to cause the messages in *Designed for Success* and *Ready, Set…Grow!* to be delivered in the right seasons.

Thank you to the sisters of my heart, Georgeanne, Judy, Kathy, Liz, Lori, Melanie, and Tish, who watch over me with prayer, support my dreams, and encourage me to press on. I cherish each of you as a precious gift in the garden of my life.

And to three special men—my father, my husband, and my son. You are mighty trees in my life. You are my shelter and my shade. You stand tall in the storm, and you anchor me. I thank God for all of you and for the opportunity to write this book, encouraging everyone who reads it to…grow!

# CONTENTS

## PART III: PRODUCING

*Every blade of grass has its Angel that bends*
*over it and whispers, "Grow—grow!"*
—THE TALMUD

S HE WAS WAITING ALONE in the hallway of a beautiful hotel in San Antonio, Texas. I will never forget her. Tears streaked her face. She waited an eternity for the crowd to clear, and the only words she could find in that moment were, "I've lost my hope." Then this single mother of two, barely more than a child herself, told me her story.

I met her again in a conference in southern California. Her words dripped with bitterness when she said, "You can work for a company for twenty-five years, and they'll kick you to the curb six months before you retire."

"I worry all of the time," she told me in a letter. "I've learned the wrong lessons in my life. I've learned to be defensive and bitter. I've forgotten how to dream."

She said in an e-mail, "I am overwhelmed on my job. I feel like I am failing, and I am so afraid of being fired."

She is beginning a new job today—an opportunity pregnant with promise. She is full of energy and the naïve idea she can make a real difference. Within three months she will sink into the disillusionment and negativity of that corporate culture. Within a year you won't recognize her.

Her mission was once clear. She now drags herself out of the door every working day to a job where she counts endless minutes. Purpose has drained from her work; what is left *at the bottom* of that cup is bitter and unsatisfying.

She has served her family faithfully for decades. Instead of feeling honored and appreciated, she feels neglected and disregarded—used up. She is afraid to hope again, because she cannot bear to be disappointed...again.

I've seen her in almost every state, in South Africa, Kenya, the United Kingdom, Australia, Tasmania, Canada, and Mexico. Each time I see her, she looks different. But some things are always the same. In her eyes there is a longing, an awareness, a glimpse of what could be. She wants to live and work differently, and she is so tired. She is weary from packing the heaviness of disappointment, rejection, responsibility, and hurt.

You may know her. One day she woke up and looked around her life. It was not what she had dreamed it would be—when she had a dream. Now her days are filled with endless obligations. Her life has become one giant "to do" list.

Every day she catches the bus, runs the errands, and crosses off the tasks. At the end of the day her mind turns with the things she didn't accomplish, but her body is so tired. She is pouring herself out, and she is empty.

You may know her—or *you may be her.*

If I could give her (or you) a gift, I would choose hope, hope that does not disappoint or perish. I would choose perennial hope to grow wild in the garden of your life. In fact, if I could, I would plant it for you.

But as with the characters we love in *The Wizard of Oz*, their long journey taught them that what they were seeking had been always been *inside* of them. So it is with you. Your hope is not lost. It is quietly resting like a rose beneath the snow waiting for the spring.

This book intends to refresh. It is gentle rain falling on the seeds of promise. It is a book for personal restoration—the taking back and taking hold of hope. Here, expectancy is likened to a rain gauge measuring the accumulation of hope.

This book is for those whose hope fell on the hard footpath and was snatched away. It for those whose hope is languishing in the sun with roots too shallow to bear the heat of life. It is for the ones who felt the stirring of hope overcome by the weight of distraction and worry. It is also for those who have become *good soil*—those who want to plant seeds of hope, even in gardens they will never sit in.

I pray this book will find its way into the arms of each person who has lost her dream or never learned how to dream; to the one who is deeply disappointed, daring not to hope for more; to the multitude who believe it is too late for them, that the time for hoping and dreaming has passed; to those whose choices have brought them to a dry and desolate place; and to women who are weary and overwhelmed by the burdens they carry. As each person reads, I pray each and every one will...

- Fully realize you were designed to live abundantly

- Stop settling for a mediocre existence

- Live in a state of anticipation, not anxiety

- Take personal responsibility and shed the victim mentality

- Discard the thorny bouquets of offense you've carried far too long

- Choose and grow positive, productive relationships

- Release toxic alliances that poison the spirit

- Identify self-limiting beliefs, attitudes, and behaviors

- Design life with challenging and realistic goals

- Cultivate optimism, even in the most difficult circumstances

- Walk in a spirit of gratitude and grace

- Develop the personal disciplines that produce hope

- Bear beautiful fruit and have real impact

*Ready, Set... Grow!* is organized in three collections—Preparation, Planting, and Producing.

The first collection will help you to clear the ground. In these chapters, you will confront the beliefs, behaviors, and even relationships that must be uprooted—the stones and stumps that must be removed in order for hope to take root. Clearing is a conscious decision to *take back* the ground you may have given over to self-limiting beliefs, learned helplessness, victim mentalities, and toxic alliances.

In the second collection, you will learn how to plant seeds of hope and positive expectancy. These seeds are the words we speak, the dreams we dare to cultivate, the disciplines we embrace, and the way we learn to "frame" life events.

The third collection carries a theme of producing—growing relationships, abilities, and confidence. Here you are encouraged to produce and perpetuate hope. These reflections focus on evaluation and adjustment, guarding against complacency, and sowing positive expectancy into others.

Following each chapter you will find a journaling exercise designed to process the ideas and make them yours. At the end of each collection, key points are summarized as "Seeds of Hope." Here you will have the opportunity to capture and prioritize action steps that will plant hope into your life and the lives of others.

What then is hope? Is it an attitude or a perspective? Is it science or faith? Is it an action, a skill, or a discipline? As we move forward, you may discover hope to be all of these things and more. Hope has many faces, and where she lives, marvelous things are possible. Hope is what makes it possible for you to assert to yourself: "I'm *ready*, I'm *set*...AND NOW I'M GOING TO *GROW!*"

I will do my best to cast the seeds, and I pray they will grow into a hope perennial.

*Part 1*

# PREPARATION

# CLEARING AND TAKING BACK YOUR GROUND

*Her desert will blossom like Eden,*
*her barren wilderness like the garden of the LORD.*
*Joy and gladness will be found there.*
*Songs of thanksgiving will fill the air.*
*—ISAIAH 51:3*

EVERY YEAR MILLIONS OF us make New Year's resolutions. We solidly resolve to eliminate every bad habit, eat healthier, exercise more, spend less, and generally become *better* human beings.

This is a perfect system because it gives us yet another opportunity to tell ourselves that next week, next month, after the holidays, and with the New Year...we will suddenly be different! We don't have to be different today.

For many of us, the resolution exercise is quite inspiring and lasts at least one week.

Then we sink back into the old ways of thinking and doing. The commitments we made are abandoned for another year. I know this because the gyms are packed on January 2. You can't find a parking space or get near a machine! (Be patient, the parking lot and the locker room will clear out in seven to ten days, and you'll have the place all to yourself.)

I also know this because I've done it too. (And I bet you can relate.)

Why don't these heartfelt changes "stick"? Why can't we get the traction we need to move forward in our lives and create positive change?

Perhaps, in part, it is because we try to plant good things on top of garbage heaps. For real and lasting change to occur, we must clear the ground and turn the soil. Before we can plant what is good into our lives, we must remove the stumps and stones.

We shouldn't expect to wake up one bright morning and be magically *different*. When we go to bed on the last night of the year, we will not miraculously wake up with new habits and disciplines! That is just ridiculous.

Preparing the ground is backbreaking, not-so-glamorous work. It requires that we dig below the surface. It requires that we realize that enduring change (and the most beautiful gardens) always grows from the inside out.

# 1

# ROOT BOUND

*Beliefs that limit you*

A ROOT-BOUND PLANT HAS RUN out of room to grow. The life-giving root system becomes so confined and twisted that it cannot bring nutrients to the vine. The same can happen with our *roots*, which are the beliefs that bind us to our current condition and shape our future.

A story that illustrates this is of a farmer who plants a large field of pumpkins. Early in the season, he walks through the rows inspecting the new crop. The pumpkins are just beginning to appear on the vine.

Thrown off to the side of the rows is a glass jar. As an experiment, he places one of the tiny pumpkins (still on the vine) inside the jar. When he returns a few weeks later, the crop is flourishing! The pumpkins have grown so much...with the exception of one. The pumpkin inside the jar has grown to fill the glass. It has completely conformed to this prison and simply run out of room to grow.

What happened to that pumpkin also happens to people. What we believe about ourselves, others, our future, and even our past will shape our growth and influence our results. If we want to grow, we must learn to break the glass of self-limiting beliefs.

*If what we believe about ourselves and what we believe about our future possibility are contained in a vessel that will not allow us to stretch and grow, we become root-bound.*

Picture yourself holding a glass jar containing your current life—a life conformed within that glass jar of your own beliefs about...

- Yourself and your abilities

- Your future and your possibilities

- Other people

- Life situations and events

As you continue reading you will learn to break the jar of self-limiting beliefs and free the roots of your potential.

It is easy for the roots of belief to become twisted and tangled. When they do, our relationships and results suffer. Unbinding the roots is a four-step process:

1. Identify the beliefs that limit you.

2. Understand how those beliefs are impacting your results and relationships. (Understanding the impact will motivate you to make the changes necessary.)

3. Exchange self-limiting beliefs for empowering ones.

4. Identify beliefs you want to add to yourself. These are possibilities you may not have considered until now, but they are possibilities. (And they can be yours.)

## IDENTIFY YOUR SELF-LIMITING BELIEFS

This is a deeply reflective exercise, one that will ask you to reach below the surface and confront deep-seated and long-standing assumptions. You will discover things about yourself you have not known, and you will understand yourself and your relationships better than ever before. There are no *right* or *wrong* answers here. This is a little excavation, a little exploration, and a whole lot of reflection.

Journaling is a great tool for this exercise. If you are not keeping a journal now, this is a marvelous reason to begin. Think of this as your personal *blog*. The entries mark your journey and become *memorial stones* you place along the way. (By the end of the exercise I hope you are absolutely hooked on the idea of blogging or journaling. It is one of the best ways to process what you discover on your journey.)

An easy way to capture and catalog your beliefs is to draw a line down the middle of a page, creating two columns. Label the first column *Empowering* and the second column *Limiting*. Now you are ready to find the beliefs that drive your life and shape your future.

## What You Believe Becomes Your Truth

Positive beliefs empower you. They lift your head. These are the beliefs that make you resilient and give you the courage to press on even in the face of adversity.

As Noelle Nelson cites in an article for *Futurist Magazine*: "Beliefs are the bedrock upon which all experience is built. Your success depends on the beliefs you hold. What you believe determines how you go about things, whether you seek out one type of situation or another, and what you are or are not willing to try. Beliefs that in the past wouldn't have held you back nowadays will."[1]

It will not surprise you to learn that the most successful people are also the most hopeful and optimistic. Their beliefs empower, energize, and embolden them. These people hold life events in that context—they evaluate what happens (even failure and hardship) differently.

Negative beliefs, on the other hand, limit you. They are the *lies* you tell yourself about yourself, about others, and the future. The big problem—the root-bound problem—is that the lies you tell yourself actually become your truth. This is what author Brian Tracy calls the "Law of Belief." Whatever you believe, with feeling, becomes your reality.[2]

This is not a new discovery. It has always been so. And it is so with you. You believe some things about yourself, others, your past, and the future that simply are not true. They have become true because you have believed something and you have acted on it. Robert K. Merton, a distinguished sociologist and Columbia University professor, was first to call this the "self-fulfilling prophecy."[3]

What do you believe about yourself, your finances, relationships, spiritual life, and health? What do you believe about your career and your future? These beliefs are writing the story of your life.

What you believe about yourself and your possibility need not be true. If you believe it, it is true for you. You will consciously and unconsciously move in that direction. Whether it is a belief about your job, finances, health, relationships, or any other important area of your life, you are steadily moving in the direction of your thoughts. Indeed, there is a prophet inside of you predicting the future.

Think of it this way: Beliefs bear thoughts. Thoughts bear words. Words inspire behaviors. And behaviors give birth to results.

The results you are getting right now, in every area of your life, reflect what you believe! If you want a new result, you must get a new belief.

I have been collecting and cataloging beliefs for some time. I find them in letters and e-mails. I listen for them as women tell me their stories. If you and I were speaking now, I would love to hear your story, and I would listen for the beliefs that are summarizing your past and shaping your future.

Here is a peek at my collection. Do any of these resonate with you?

| Empowering Beliefs | Limiting Beliefs |
| --- | --- |
| I am learning and growing every day. | I am too old to start over or learn new things. |
| I am beautiful. | I don't fit in. |
| I like myself. | It is very important for others to approve of me. |
| I do many things well. | I am not very talented. |

| Empowering Beliefs | Limiting Beliefs |
|---|---|
| My future is full of possibility. | If I expect too much, I'll be disappointed. |
| I try new approaches. | I can't afford to take any chances. |
| I am a valuable resource to my employer. | I am just one small person in a huge company. |
| I can make a real difference for others. | People will take advantage of you. |
| I have accomplished many things. | I haven't achieved anything of real importance. |
| I can profit even from failure. | Failure is not an option. |
| Opportunity is waiting for me. | I am afraid of the future. |
| It is important to take care of myself. | It is selfish to take care of myself. |
| I have many options. | If I blow this opportunity, I don't know what I'll do. |
| I believe my future is secure. | There are no guarantees in life. |
| I expect to be successful. | I don't deserve to be successful. |
| I am blessed. | Good things don't last. |

There is a remarkable difference between these two lists, and I guarantee there is a huge difference in the results they inspire. As you read on, you will see how beliefs on both sides of this table impact our behaviors and, ultimately, our results.

But first you are ready to discover the beliefs operating below the surface at your roots.

Begin by listening to what you say *to yourself* and what you say *about yourself*. These thoughts and statements reflect what you believe about you—who you are and what you are capable of. For example when you say, "I can't," "I've never been good at…," or "I am afraid…," reach behind the words to find the belief and write it down in the limiting beliefs column.

When you think, "I can," "I am getting better at…," or "I am excited about…," capture the beliefs in the empowering column.

As you gather your beliefs, you will probably find some *outdated self-perceptions.* Perceptions become outdated when you have changed or grown, but you don't recognize it. When you look in the mirror or reflect on your life, you still see the *old you.* When you talk to yourself or about yourself, you tell an *old story.* The old story draws you in and shapes your decisions and your expectations.

Outdated self-perceptions also occur when you suspect a positive change is really a temporary condition. A good example is the weight-loss *yo-yo* many women ride. (Like a yo-yo, we move up and down on the scale and in our dress size.) One woman explained it to me this way: "My closet is not arranged by seasons; it is arranged by sizes! I have everything in there from a size 6 to a size 16!" That's not only expensive and space consuming—it is also unhealthy and exhausting!

Here's where a faulty belief system comes into play. I can punish my body with some strange fad-of-a-diet and lose the weight. The problem is, as I slip victoriously into my size 6, I am still thinking like a size 16!

I am not a size 6 in my own mind. I am a size 16, posing like a 6. I am an imposter! Even as people tell me how great I look, I am terrified of losing my victory. I know that I am one cheeseburger away from riding that scale all the way back up!

In this example, I cannot hold on to my success because I don't really expect to. There is a part of me that fully expects to gain the weight back. In fact, I don't throw away the larger sizes because I expect to wear them again. And that is exactly what happens.

As one woman put it: "I believe I can lose weight, and I believe I can gain weight. I just don't believe I can maintain my ideal weight." (And until now in her life she has been absolutely right!)

Outdated self-perceptions are just one example of self-limiting beliefs. There are others, and I encourage you to find every limiting belief that is operating in your life. In the pages to come you will learn where to look for them and what to do once you find them.

Notice, for example, what you say and believe about your future.

Questions like these will help you isolate what you believe is in store for you:

- What do you say and think about the future?

- What do you expect as you begin a new day?

- What are you bracing yourself for?

- What are you afraid will happen?

- What are you worrying about?

## CHECK YOUR GLASSES AND UPDATE YOUR FRAMES

Do you believe the future contains amazing possibilities for you, or are you frightened of what the future may bring? If we walk in fear of the future rather than in confidence, fear becomes the lens through which we look. With that perspective, we will naturally respond to the perceived threat, not the opportunity of a situation.

*Problems are magnified when you look through glasses of fear.*

A woman wrote to me recently asking for advice about a challenging job situation. In her midfifties, she worried that she could not keep up with new technologies and processes. The theme of her letter was absolute, crippling fear. She was afraid of failing, of being fired, of not having the skills to find a new job, and ultimately of losing everything she had worked for.

Keep in mind, none of this had actually happened—she was just afraid that it would. She had managed to thoroughly *catastrophize* the situation. Like a snowball rolling down a hill, her fear was growing and building momentum. It was, in fact, overtaking her. Through the lens of fear, every change at work looked insurmountable, any word of correction sounded like judgment, and the smallest mistake felt like complete failure.

She ended her letter by asking, "What can I do?"

My answer was fairly straightforward. "You must change what you believe about yourself and your future and evict fear from your life."

Once you have identified what you believe about you and your future, investigate what you expect from and believe about others. These are important clues to help you manage relationships and understand your responses.

In my book *Designed for Success,* we explored how we limit relationships and results by the labels we place on others. Once I label you, I will look for and notice everything that lines up with that label, and I will dismiss or ignore what does not. I will search for and validate what I already believe is true.[4]

Let's say I have labeled you as "Defensive" based on our past communications. Today I need to speak with you about something. It's not a big deal, but I know you will make it a big deal, because that is what you do. As I approach you, I see the word *DEFENSIVE* tattooed in giant capital letters across your forehead. (For good measure, I mentally underline that. Now you are <u>DEFENSIVE</u>.)

Physically, I brace myself for your defensive response. (That's fair. We've been here before, and I'm not an idiot.) As I approach you, my heart beats faster, my body is rigid, and my facial expression probably reflects my expectation ("This is going to get ugly"). My brow is furrowed, my jaw is tight, and if I am able to force a smile, it will be through tightly clenched teeth!

What does all that look like to you?

You might say it looks like an attack, and in that case your natural response will be to defend.

We have our discussion, and it does become confrontational. I walk away thinking, "That woman is so rigidly DEFENSIVE!"

Everything I expected from you has come true—not because you are defensive, but because I acted on my expectation that you would be. I reached in and pulled that behavior out of you! (It's a pretty neat trick, isn't it?)

It is absolutely true. What you believe about and expect from others you will search for and even reinforce. In the example above, if I want to change the pattern of my communication with you, I must remove the negative label. The communication cannot and will not change until the label or the expectation does.

Take a moment to assess the relationships in your personal and professional life.

- Are some relationships showing signs of strain?

- Are there people you have trouble communicating with or getting results from?

- What are you expecting from these people?

- What do you believe about them?

- How are those expectations and beliefs reflected in your voice, tone, and posture?

- In what ways are your expectations becoming self-fulfilling prophecies?

- How are your beliefs limiting your relationships and your results with others?

As you work through these reflective exercises, you may find the *Limiting* list growing longer than the *Empowering* list. If so, celebrate! That means you are locating what is holding you back, and you are one step closer to moving those obstacles out of the way.

The beliefs operating in your life were planted by you, by others, and by your experiences over time. Through this exercise you have seen how they have taken hold and how they have promoted (released) or stunted (confined) your growth or personal potential.

You are not finished with your lists! It is time to exchange your self-limiting beliefs for ones that will empower and infuse you with hope and expectancy. In this process you will need to be patient. This exchange will not happen magically or instantly. It is a process that will unfold as you read on.

## Journaling Exercise

Locating the self-limiting beliefs is the first step to unbinding your roots. That is the excavation. Once you have done that, take the time to reflect on how these assumptions help or harm you. Explore the impact they have on your life. Review your list and ask yourself:

1. What behaviors do these beliefs invite?
2. How do they push me forward or hold me back?
3. What do these beliefs cause me to think about and focus on?
4. How do they make me feel?
5. How did I acquire these beliefs?

When you take the time to answer questions like these, something very important will begin to happen. At a very conscious level you will understand your responses, and that empowers you to make the changes you would like to see. You recognize the beliefs, understand their impact, and purposefully work to create a new context for yourself.

# 2

# EXPERIENCE CAN BE
# A BAD TEACHER

*Rewriting history when you've
learned the wrong lesson*

S HARON IS A MOTHER of two young boys. Her marriage has just
ended, and she is devastated by the betrayal of an unfaithful
husband. Sharon learned not to trust and how to hate. Without
realizing it or meaning to, she is passing those lessons along to her
children. That may be the most devastating result of all.

The lessons we learn are the ones we share. *When we learn the
wrong lesson, we will teach it to others. We pass along a dysfunctional legacy.*

An event or experience does not have the power to shape our
expectations. It is the way we interpret and process the event that
does that—how we summarize it, how we tell the story, and what we
remember about it. It is what we replay in our brain that ultimately
carves the memory into our minds.

My son grew up throwing a baseball from the time he was four
years old through his senior year at Oklahoma Baptist University.
One of the best examples of learning the wrong lesson, I learned
from him.

We moved from Colorado Springs, Colorado, to San Antonio,
Texas, in Tabor's second year of high school. His first game with the
new team was a large tournament in Houston. When he returned
from this weekend trip, he was absolutely crestfallen. When I asked
him how it went, he announced, "They rocked my world."

Moving into motivational *mama* mode, I said, "Buck up, pal. You will have days like that. You can't let one bad game throw your confidence. Shake it off, and get back in the game."

He looked at me and said, "You don't understand. I had a great day. They hit everything I've got."

For three weeks, his game was totally off. Finally, his coach said to me, "You're the motivational speaker—do something!"

Not quite sure what to do, I asked my son what he was thinking about now when he was on the pitcher's mound. He told me he was thinking about Houston. Then I understood: He was replaying that game over and over in his mind. He was quite literally reliving it!

We immediately went home and pulled out the box all good mothers have. (You know the box, with every wonderful thing your child has ever said or done.) We reviewed the baseball articles, awards, and victories. We talked about the wins and the saves. Almost immediately, my son remembered how to pitch. It was a baseball miracle!

He went on to have a fabulous pitching record through high school and college (which included pitching a perfect game his senior year of college).

My son learned the wrong lesson in Houston. He learned that he was out of his league or that he might not have what it takes on this new team. The real lesson—the right lesson—was that he was competing at a new level. His skills would be stretched, and he would grow.

The wrong lesson demoralized him and stole his confidence. The right lesson challenged and motivated him. It ignited his passion for the game.

Through that experience, I understood how important it is to take the *right* lessons from our experiences—even the setbacks and disappointments. The wrong lessons demotivate and paralyze us. The right lessons inspire, equip, and encourage us to move beyond the disappointment into the victory.

How do you know if you've learned the wrong lesson? There is an easy test. *Wrong lessons take something from you. Right lessons add something to you.*

If I could live my life over, there are so many things I would do differently! Can you relate to that? That's not regret speaking; it is perspective. I shake my head at some of the mistakes and choices I made. What was I thinking! Why didn't I see and exercise my options?

To some degree, it is because those mistakes and experiences created insight (and hopefully a bit of wisdom). I learned from them, just as you have learned from your past. And perhaps you and I did the best we could with the tools, information, skills, and faith we had at the time. Rather than beat ourselves with remnants of the past—with a list of should haves and shouldn't haves—we can pull the lessons out and profit from the experiences.

Take a moment to think about your setbacks, disappointments, and failures. What are the lessons you took from those experiences? How did those events (and the lessons you learned through them) impact your next attempts? How are they still impacting you?

Here are some classic examples of taking away the wrong lesson. In each of these events, the lesson learned will rob the *student* of a future victory. This is profound when you understand that the event actually perpetuates itself by the lesson learned.

- An employee's idea is not implemented; she stops offering suggestions.

- A job candidate is not selected for a position; she concludes it was a political decision and she didn't have a chance anyway.

- A performance review is negative; an employee learns to defend, explain, and blame others for disappointing results.

- Sales are dramatically down; a top-producing sales-person begins to doubt her ability.

The biggest problem with learning the wrong lesson is the behavior it inspires and the beliefs it plants. *Bad* lessons are often the seeds that grow into self-limiting beliefs.

Let's look at the list again.

1. When an employee's ideas are not implemented, she can rewrite history by studying her approach and presenting her ideas differently in the future. She can also set realistic expectations. Not every idea will be implemented, just as every ball won't be knocked out of the park. Even so, you keep looking for the strikes, and you swing for the bleachers!

2. When a candidate is not selected for a position, she can ask for feedback and learn how to be more prepared for the next opportunity. She can also learn how to build her professional network and market her results more effectively.

3. If a performance review is negative, an employee can learn to manage her feedback, demonstrate personal accountability, and build an action plan to improve the results.

4. When a salesperson is disappointed by her results, she can evaluate her approaches and sharpen her skills. She can enlist the help of a mentor and explore new ways of attracting business.

In every event, there is something to be learned, especially from the disappointments, failures, and setbacks. We have choices about what we take away from those experiences. As you can see from the examples above, what we choose to learn is important.

*Ultimately, the lesson is more important than the event.*

It's interesting to note that organizations can learn the wrong lessons too. One of the best examples is how companies cripple themselves with bureaucracy. Every organization I work with can relate to miles of red tape and layers of bureaucracy.

If I want to hear a spontaneous *corporate groan*, I simply ask the audience, "Is there any bureaucracy around here?" With that question I can guarantee a unanimous groan throughout the room. Without a doubt, bureaucracy is one of the most frustrating things employees deal with on a daily basis. With an insatiable appetite, it consumes time, resources, and energy.

In his book *Good to Great*, Jim Collins writes that bureaucracy is created to compensate for a lack of discipline or skill.[1] For example, when mistakes are made, organizations often respond by creating another layer of *supervision* or adding more hoops for employees to jump through.

Instead of building more skill and discipline, we add rules and policies and procedures. We create another report or a form to fill out in triplicate. Ultimately we end up checking the checkers who check the checkers. With that mentality, productivity comes to a grinding halt and costs climb through the roof!

I once heard a story about a small town with a beautiful park. The park was a pristine, natural resource. The city fathers decided they must protect the park from vandalism and harm, so they hired a park steward to watch over it.

Before too long, they realized the park steward would need shelter—a place to escape the weather. They built him a booth, and all was well.

But wait! Once there was a facility in the park, they needed a facilities manager. One was hired immediately. Now with a park steward and a facilities manager, the city needed someone to oversee this staff. A manager was hired.

When the city went through the annual budgeting process, there was a shortfall of funds. They simply did not have enough money in the budget, so they fired the park steward!

This story illustrates what I see all too often. We wander far from the original intention when we learn the wrong lessons and lose sight of the real business objectives.

When employees groan about bureaucracy, I tell them to get over it. We will never completely eliminate bureaucracy. That isn't our job, and quite frankly it is out of our control. Our only hope is to make it absolutely unnecessary. We do that by developing more skill and discipline.

*We don't eliminate bureaucracy; we make it irrelevant.*

So, personally and corporately, it is quite possible to learn the wrong lessons from our experiences. When that happens, we limit and constrain the future. Our results won't reflect what is possible until we learn the right lessons.

## Journaling Exercise

This is a good time to review your list of self-limiting beliefs.

1. Which of them were planted in your heart and mind through a disappointment, setback, or failure?

2. What events have shaped your beliefs and perceptions?

3. Have you "learned" the wrong lessons from your experience?

4. If you were to "rewrite history" or retell that story, what are the "right" or "real" lessons?

# 3

# HELPLESS BECOMES HOPELESS

*If you are learning to be helpless, you*
*are learning to be hopeless*

OUR SOCIETY ENCOURAGES PEOPLE to think and behave like victims in dozens of ways. When we create a culture of entitlement and reward low accountability, we actually teach people how to be helpless! This is a tragedy, because in learning to be helpless, we also learn to be hopeless.

Have you noticed that somewhere along the line it actually became fashionable and trendsetting to be a victim? On the surface, this is wonderful because we are not responsible for our attitudes, behaviors, and results. Thank goodness—our bad behavior, our mistakes, and poor decisions are not our fault! We are like we are because: our parents were strict...our teachers were cruel...our friends teased us when we were in grade school...we didn't know better...we were tricked into it!

If those excuses don't work, we can always blame our genes. We are stubborn because we come from a long line of very stubborn people. We are hotheaded and short-tempered because it's in our blood!

I love what Stephen Covey has to say on this in his timeless work *The 7 Habits of Highly Effective People.* "Don't argue for other people's weaknesses. Don't argue for your own. When you make a mistake, admit it, correct it, and learn from it—immediately. Don't get into a blaming, accusing mode. Work on things you have control over. Work on you. On *me.*"[1]

*Public Service Announcement:
You are not a victim of your past, your
present, or your genes. You do have choices
and options. You can empower yourself,
even in the most difficult situations. In the
end, it is not what happens to you; it is how
you respond that will become the story of
your life.*

Learned helplessness is a theory attributed to Dr. Martin Seligman.[2] We learn to be helpless when we come to believe that we have no control over our situation. When we believe we do not have the power to change what is happening to us, we become passive. In this passive place we do not exercise our options, protect our boundaries, or empower ourselves to make change. We simply accept.

A simple illustration of learned helplessness is the elephant in a traveling road show. When the elephant is very young, trainers place a band or bracelet on a back ankle. For several hours each day the elephant is leashed to a heavy metal rod cemented into the ground. At first the elephant will pull and struggle, but without success. He is not able to pull free. He cannot lift the tethered foot. Eventually the elephant will *adapt* and learn to move about while keeping the leashed foot firmly planted to the ground.

The elephant grows into a powerful animal, and the show goes on the road. In a field somewhere in Middle America, he is tethered to a stake that is simply hammered into the ground. He could walk away easily, but he won't because he has learned to be helpless in this situation. He has been conditioned to believe that when tethered to the stake, he cannot pick up his foot.

*Learned helplessness is the reaction of giving up because we do not believe anything we can do will make a difference.*

People learn helplessness too. We learn to be helpless when we believe (mistakenly or not) that we have no control over a situation. Unfortunately, when we learn to be helpless in one set of circumstances, we may carry that forward in the next and the next.

Another condition that feeds the victim mentality and helplessness is self-centeredness. It's interesting to note that people with personality disorders have many things in common. At the top of that list is lack of individual accountability, which results in a victim mentality and blaming others, society, and the universe for their problems![3] We simply cannot afford that attitude to leech into the soil of our lives. It is toxic and will poison our minds, our relationships, our results, and our hope.

At work, people with a victim mentality spend their time looking outside of themselves to explain what happened or didn't happen. These people tend to be very good "documenters." They are always documenting something or someone just in case they need to justify their case. Frankly, this exhausts me. (I'm thinking, "If you were to work as hard at your job as you work at the documentation, you might not need so much documentation!")

At home, the victim might sound like a martyr. "I am the only one who does anything around here. No one lifts a finger to help. My family doesn't appreciate me." (Incidentally, if I am playing the role of martyr, I probably won't ask for—or accept—help. If someone were to help me, I risk losing my beautiful martyr badge.)

Sharon, an administrative professional for a legal practice, is (in her words) a "recovered victim." She recognized what it was costing her to be a victim and has reclaimed her personal power. "Unconsciously, I would set people up," she admits. "I volunteered for projects and then complained about being overworked. I offered to do things for people, only to resent being taken advantage of. I was looking for recognition, but instead I developed a very negative reputation. I lost a lot of credibility, and people didn't trust me."

The victim mentality impacts hope on many levels:

1. When I think like a victim, I am planting and feeding beliefs that limit me.

2. If I see myself as victim, someone or something must be to blame. Blame becomes my focus. This damages trust.

3. Because I am drawing the wrong lessons from my experiences, I am learning to be helpless in the future.

4. If I learn to be helpless, I am likely to teach to it others. I drain others of their hope.

In the most devastating circumstances, some people focus on what they cannot do and what they have lost. Others focus on what they can control and what they have. Incredibly, those who lose the most are often the most triumphant. What remains (even in the rubble) is a beautiful, relentless hope for the future.

This transcends resilience. It is so much more than bouncing back from disaster or disappointment. They see the disaster and disappointment though hopeful eyes. Regardless of the circumstances, these are the people who refuse to let go of hope. They cling to hope even more tightly in the storm.

Just after the devastation left by Hurricane Katrina, I was speaking in Dallas, Texas. The hotels were filled to overflowing with people who had lost everything. I had a chance to speak with many of them, and I will always remember one gentleman I heard on an early morning radio show.

With a home completely destroyed, this man and his family fled New Orleans and were living in a Dallas shelter. On this morning a reporter asked him, "What will you do now?"

His answer was remarkable. He said, "This morning my family and I will serve breakfast here. We lost what we own, but we still have what we are. We are strong and healthy. We want to help." He went on to say, "If you are an employer, I'd like to introduce myself. I am a good worker. I have a family of five to feed, and I'd like to start right away."

That is not the voice of a victim! This is the sound of character and hope and personal accountability. This man knows a secret, and he is teaching it to his children. Sometimes terrible, devastating things happen. When they do, you may need help, but even then you are not helpless. (By the way, this man received dozens of job offers within hours, and I think whoever hired him hit the jackpot.)

Social anthropologists study the aftermath of such disasters to understand how people experience and explain what happens to them. Because disasters do not care if you are young or old, rich or poor, events like Katrina are called the "great equalizers." What begins as an even playing field is quickly changed by the way people respond.

What is the antidote for learned helplessness? The gentleman in the story above demonstrated it beautifully. It is service.

Service is a powerful strategy to reclaim hope and counter the sense of learned helplessness. In studies concerning at-risk and troubled youth, volunteering proves to be one of the most successful therapies. Statistics show a clear correlation between volunteering and reducing risky behavior.[4] When we reach out to meet a real human need, our focus shifts from *poor me* to *empowered me*. Instead of feeling powerless, I am, in fact, powerful enough to make a difference.

What a wonderful belief to acquire. I am powerful enough to make a difference! While you're at it, perhaps you want to add the belief that you always have options; even in the most difficult times of your life, you have something of value to give. Maybe you'll add the belief that you can make a big difference. I hope as you read this that you will begin to believe you can actually change the world. That would most certainly belong in the *Empowering* column.

## JOURNALING EXERCISE

To this point we have talked a great deal about exchanging the beliefs that limit for those that empower. I encourage you to look at your lists again. This time look for beliefs you want to add to the *Empowering* column of your life.

1. What beliefs to you want to acquire?

2. If you add these beliefs to your *Empowering* column, how will your life change?

3. What could prevent you from making these acquisitions?

# 4

# REJECTING REJECTION

*The roots of rejection lie deep within ourselves*

OR MORE THAN TWO years I battled a painful, nearly debilitating skin condition on the palms of my hands. I tried special diets, medicines, creams, ointments, and strange home remedies. Nothing worked, and the diagnosis was not hopeful. Apparently this was an autoimmune disease with no known cure. That was definitely not the answer I was looking for, and I set out to find another one.

After months of reading everything I could find, I stumbled upon the answer. I knew it was my answer because it created such a profound emotional response. This revelation not only hit me; it knocked me right over. I literally lost my legs for a moment, and I wept for hours.

I learned there is a direct link between autoimmune diseases (like the skin disorder I had) and self-rejection. It makes perfect sense. If I reject myself, I should not be surprised when my body turns upon itself, literally attacking from within.

*People who reject themselves have chronic feelings of unworthiness. What happens on the outside of us is often a clue about what is happening on the inside of us.*

As Dr. Don Colbert teaches, many diseases have spiritual roots. We are mind, body, and spirit. "Although traditional medicine often sees these facets of our being as separate, in truth they are not. A vital link exists between the spirit, soul, and body."[1]

I have struggled with that sense of unworthiness for much of my life. People are sometimes surprised by that. When I admit it, they almost always say, "You?"

Yes, me. But for the first time, I was physically and quite visibly confronted by what Dr. Colbert calls a "deadly emotion." This was no longer something I could hide or cover up with a smile. I could not slap on my *happy mask* and perform, pretending to be the perfect picture of confidence and control. I even thought, "Why does it have to be my hands? Why couldn't it be somewhere easier to hide?"

Isn't that interesting? The first response may be to *cover* the condition rather than *confront* it.

To see if self-rejection is a problem for you, check the box beside each statement that describes you:

- ☐ No matter how hard I work or what I achieve, I could have done better.

- ☐ When others praise me, deep down I don't really believe them.

- ☐ At some level I fear that if people really knew me, they wouldn't accept me.

- ☐ I've done some bad stuff, and I have a difficult time forgiving myself.

- ☐ When good things happen, I often feel undeserving or unworthy.

- ☐ It is easy to give but difficult to accept from others.

- ☐ I spend a lot of time thinking about or worrying about what others think of me.

- ☐ It is very important to please others (and difficult to feel good about myself if others aren't pleased with me).

- ☐ I worry too much about how I look.

☐ I am too sensitive and too easily hurt.

☐ I hear the criticism of others even when they insist that was not the intended message.

☐ I often feel inferior, inadequate, and out of place.

☐ It is hard for me to trust—myself, others, or even God.

☐ I feel better when I am in complete control.

☐ I tend to dominate situations (because that gives me a sense of control).

☐ Even though I don't always express it, I often feel critical, frustrated, or angry toward others.

☐ I tend to isolate myself from others.

☐ I often miss the mark, falling short of my own expectations.

☐ I carry around feelings of guilt and shame.

How many of these do you recognize in yourself? Is self-rejection a problem for you? If it is, how is it revealed in your relationships, your results, and even your health?

## WHY DO WE REJECT OURSELVES?

Self-rejection is grafted from two of the most painful of human experiences—rejection and shame. When these have taken root in our lives, we can become desperately tangled in what we should have done, what we shouldn't have done, or what shouldn't have happened...and did.

Shame can grow from the seed of guilt. We may deeply regret the mistakes of our past and—even though we may be forgiven—may not have managed to forgive ourselves. Even thinking about what we have done or failed to do creates a shame response. We are angry with ourselves and feel unworthy or undeserving of good things (because deep down we are *bad*).

Shame is also created by things that happen to us—things that *should not* have happened. We may believe what happened is somehow our fault. A classic example of this is domestic abuse. Over time, women who are battered may actually begin to believe they are to blame. Somehow they deserved the abuse, and they must *try* harder to please the abuser.

Shame has a voice. She whispers crippling messages in your ear. Her messages sound like blame: "You are bad, you should have known better, and you don't deserve to be happy." Shame climbs onto your back, stoops your shoulders, and makes every step an effort. She pushes your head down and causes you to fold in on yourself. She makes you want to hide.

Self-rejection may have roots of shame. When you dig deeper, you may find the seed cause was the act or feeling of being rejected by others.

The rejection may be as real as abandonment or the fear of being abandoned. We can be abandoned physically or emotionally, and the fear of being abandoned is as devastating as the actual experience. In *The 7 Habits of Highly Effective People*, Stephen Covey gave us three needs of every human soul—the need to be validated, appreciated, and understood.[2] Rejection violates all three of these needs simultaneously. It is devastating.

I once had the opportunity to visit a home for *crack babies*. These are infants who have been born with drug additions because their mothers were drug-dependent during pregnancy.

Volunteers to this house have one job: rock the babies to comfort them through drug withdrawal. I will always remember one baby the volunteers called, "Precious." She was absolutely breathtaking. Her eyebrows were perfect, and they framed the most gorgeous eyes I have ever looked into. But Precious did not look back.

No matter how much I tried to make eye contact with this child, she would not. Her brow might rise as if interested in the game I was playing or the song I was singing, but she would not look into my eyes.

A nurse described this condition as a form of attachment disorder. Precious had been abandoned by an addicted mother, not once, but twice. The nurse explained that the baby would not make eye contact because eye contact is a human connection. At the age of eighteen months, her experiences with rejection taught her not to connect with another human being. "She might smile for you," the nurse said, "but she will not meet your eyes."

Thankfully, for people like Precious there is hope. What rejection steals from us can be restored. We can learn to trust again. (Wherever you are now, Precious, I pray your wounds have healed and that you are deeply loved.)

Rejection might originate from a physical deformity, abuse, or criticism. In fact, if you trace the lines from the deepest emotional wounds, you may find the source is rejection. It is not the experience of rejection that causes us to reject ourselves. It is our response to the rejection. Our confidence may be stripped away, and we actually begin to believe we are *unlovable* or undeserving of love. If we allow those deep emotional hurts to define and isolate us, the rejection moves from the outside of us to the inside of us.

*The process you are working through now allows you to pull the rejection out. It does not belong inside of you!*

Sandra's encounter with rejection is a classic example of how we set ourselves up to be rejected. "My self-esteem was at rock bottom; to protect myself from the inevitable rejection, I pushed people away," she realizes now. "I was unapproachable in how I carried myself and responded to others. I was negative, defensive, and critical. All of these attitudes and behaviors put me in solitary confinement, and that is a very lonely place."

This is a vicious cycle. When we have been rejected, we may build walls of protection. Those barriers don't *insulate*; they *isolate*. We aren't approachable, so people turn away, and we count that as yet another rejection. So, we add another brick to the wall! If you recognize this pattern in your life and relationships, I encourage you to check your own behaviors, attitudes, and responses toward others. Is there something you are doing to *set up* the rejection? If so, what needs to change in your approach so you can develop and enjoy healthy relationships?

Sandra focused on smiling more and acknowledging others. She stood taller and opened her posture. She unfolded arms that had become so accustomed to sitting across her chest and concentrated on making eye contact. She understood that her lack of confidence and self-esteem was the real problem. "The problem wasn't *out there*," she realizes now. She points to her heart as she says, "The problem was *in here*." The moment Sandra was able to own that, she was able to do something about it. She successfully reversed the cycle of rejection by pulling down the walls of defense.

This wasn't easy, but it was worth it! I encourage you to do the hard emotional work here—from the inside out. Until you do, your relationships and results will be scarred by the mark of old wounds.

## STEPS TO OVERCOMING SELF-REJECTION

If self-rejection is a problem for you, how do you overcome it?

You have already taken the most important step: acknowledging the problem. Next, you must learn to believe and authentically feel that you do belong, you are worthy of love and success, and you are capable. In a radio message on the topic of self-rejection, Charles Stanley outlines three steps to move from self-rejection to self-acceptance.

1. Identify and confront the feelings of rejection.

2. Reject the feelings of rejection.

3. Affirm yourself.[3]

In the first step, you must dig below the surface to locate and confront the feelings of rejection. (This is the not-so-glamorous part.) Here are six ways to isolate feelings of rejection.

### 1. Use a journal.

Again, my plea for journaling! It is one of the best ways to get in touch with yourself and your feelings. It takes discipline, but if you will stick with it, you will be surprised at what you learn. Over time you will notice trends in how you feel and in the events that trigger those feelings.

### 2. Pull it up by the roots.

If you know where the rejection was planted, you must pull it up by the roots. Consider writing a letter to the source of the rejection. This may be a very hard letter to write and one you may never send. That isn't the point. The purpose of your letter is to get the poison out of you and onto the page. Write your letter in an assertive, nonjudgmental way. The goal of your letter is not to assign blame. It is to confront the rejection and its impact on your life.

Below is a communication model you can use to frame your message.

When_____happened, I felt_____. The impact on my life has been_____. What I needed (or need now) is_____.

### 3. Pay attention to your feelings.

Pay attention not only to what you feel but also to why you feel that way. For example, if you feel hurt by something a friend said, reach below the hurt to find the source of the pain. Is it really what was said that hurt you? Or did the words touch a sensitive spot? (Sensitive spots are often points of low confidence and self-esteem.)

**4. Accept responsibility.**

Accept responsibility for your mistakes. Learn from them, and let them go. Your mistakes, as much as your successes, have shaped you. Perhaps they aren't *badges* of honor, but they are choices that have created perspective, wisdom, and even the capacity to forgive and understand others.

**5. Find a confidante.**

Confide in someone you can trust, someone who will tell you the truth and will not judge you. This is a person who can help you untangle the knots of rejection and help you put things into perspective.

**6. It's not about you!**

Remember, when people are negative, critical, or judgmental toward you, they are revealing themselves. That behavior speaks to *who they are*, not who you are. It's not about you! Repeat after me until you believe it: "This is not about me. I am valuable, capable, and worthy of success."

## RENOUNCE REJECTION

After identifying the source of rejection, you need to renounce it. Do that by declaring aloud: "I do not accept this rejection. I will not allow it to grow in my life." If that makes you feel silly, get over it. The words you speak have tremendous power—more power than you can even grasp. Death and life truly are in the power of the tongue (Prov. 18:21).

The last step is to replace the rejection with acceptance and affirmation. Again, these are words you speak aloud—more than once or twice. In a later chapter, you will learn more about the power of the blessing and how to affirm yourself. In the meantime, we will take a closer look at what chips away at our self-esteem and keeps us from living and loving more fully.

## JOURNALING EXERCISE

1. In what ways are you rejecting yourself?
2. How has rejection impacted what you believe about yourself, others, and your possibility?
3. What is the best way for you to confront the rejection?

# 5

# SHALLOW GROUND

*Approval, comparison, perfectionism,*
*and other common snares*

D O YOU HAVE THE perfectionist gene? I do. Here is a perfectionist's confession. (Please keep in mind this is a confession, not a tip.) I want my bathroom towels carefully folded with perfectly even edges and no tags showing. (Just between us, I spray my towels with Egyptian linen spray so they will actually smell like cotton.)

I travel extensively, and my family would attempt to help around the house when I was gone. This help included doing the laundry (bless their hearts). When I returned from trips, I would find towels randomly and carelessly stuffed in linen closets throughout the house. Because this is absolutely unacceptable, I would fluff the towels in the dryer, carefully refold, tuck in the tags, and lightly spritz them.

Seeing this, my family concluded there was no need to help with the laundry. After all, I would just redo it upon my return. So they stopped helping. Do you know what I quickly learned as the laundry piled up? Towels work great right out of the dryer!

I learned to get over it.

At the core, perfectionism feeds a need to control things and people. I have noticed something about others and myself. When we feel out of control of the big things, we may try to overcontrol small ones. In doing so, we drive ourselves (and everyone else) crazy, and, ultimately, we do nothing to impact the *big* things that still feel out of control.

To some degree, I think this explains micromanagers. These are people who suck the life out of the workforce by overmanaging the smallest details of the business. As I study that behavior, it almost always comes down to fear. Micromanagers are afraid of failing or of losing face. Or, as one self-confessed (recovering) micromanager confessed, "I am afraid people will pull something over on me and get away with it!"

Fear drives micromanagers to control. Overcontrolling is a great demotivator—it is counteractive and will never draw the best out of people. That is the great paradox. What motivates people is feeling trusted and respected, not controlled.

Perfectionism is certainly one of the traps we can fall into. Comparison is another. The nasty truth about comparison is you can never win the game. There will always be someone who has more money, a bigger house, or a nicer car. There will always be people who you think are more beautiful or talented, people who can sing better, run faster, or throw farther!

When we compare ourselves to others, we are keeping score. That means there will be a winner, and there will be a loser. When you win, I lose. I can't celebrate your victories or share in your successes. I cannot authentically support you, because if you are successful, I feel less successful. I may even be tempted to undermine you, because in the comparison game, winning is so important.

Comparison isolates us and robs us of the opportunity to invest ourselves in others. It ushers in jealousy. Incidentally, jealousy is never about what another person has, is, or does. Jealousy is a mirror reflecting a perceived deficit inside of ourselves. The next time you feel a twinge of jealousy, look squarely into that mirror and confront it!

The third snare is approval. Many of us struggle with an addiction to approval, and some of us probably need an approval intervention! When we seek the approval of others, we are looking for a way to validate ourselves. Validation is a healthy human need, but approval is not the best way to meet it.

When approval becomes your primary form of validation, it is quite possible to lose yourself. You become so preoccupied with what others think of you that you forget to think for yourself. You forget how to say no. You abandon your boundaries. When the goal becomes approval, you risk your integrity. In trying to become all things to all people, it is possible to forget who you are and what you stand for. That's when you become irrelevant.

The insatiable need for approval, constant comparison to others, and striving for perfection are all symptoms of a deeper problem—low self-esteem. This is something women often struggle with, and it kills hope. (It also kills relationships, productivity, credibility, and personal effectiveness.)

People with low self-esteem tend to be more negative, critical, and defensive. They also have a difficult time adapting to change, taking risks, and accepting feedback. Nothing on this list is attractive or empowering!

The National Association for Self-Esteem (NASE) calls self-esteem an achievement—a process that empowers, energizes, and motivates. "It is not something we have, but the experience of things we do."[1] NASE provides a comprehensive list of low self-esteem signals. Use this list to assess your own self-esteem. People with low self-esteem:

1. Are preoccupied with themselves. They spend a great deal of time thinking about and analyzing themselves.

2. Are often alienated from authority figures in life, like parents or caregivers.

3. Do not smile readily.

4. Feel tired and unmotivated.

5. Isolate themselves from others.

6. Have trouble with relationships.

7. Find eye contact uncomfortable.

8. Avoid risk.

9. Are often described as high maintenance and needy.

10. Create negative experiences.[2]

Low self-esteem plays a role in depression, addictions, eating disorders, teenage pregnancy, violence, and the list goes on. There is massive research on this topic. Here are a few statistics that hammer home how important this issue really is—for ourselves, our families, and our communities.

- Girls are more likely to be critical of themselves. In one study, 25 percent of older girls reported that they did not like or hated themselves.[3]

- The average model is 5 feet 10 inches tall and weighs 110 pounds. The average woman is 5 feet 4 inches tall and weighs 142 pounds. This discrepancy is the largest that has ever existed between women and the cultural ideal.[4]

- In the United States, approximately 10 percent of girls and women (numbering up to ten million) are suffering from diagnosed eating disorders. Of these, at least fifty thousand will die as a direct result.[5]

Reportedly, women are generally more dissatisfied with their bodies than men. I've heard that when women look in the mirror, they see themselves ten pounds heavier than they actually are. When men look at women, they see them ten pounds lighter! (This is good news for the ladies! If you've been trying to lose ten pounds, relax! You're already there, at least from the gentlemen's perspective.)

Especially in Western cultures, society has embraced *thin* as the most desirable body type. From a very young age, women are bombarded with images and pictures of how we are *supposed* to look. This is a great concern, because that *boyish, tube-like* body image is described as unhealthy and unrealistic for many women.[6] We're taught that we should look like Barbie, but if Barbie were life-sized, her organs wouldn't fit in her body!

You can see the problem here. If we evaluate our physical appearance against an impossible and unrealistic standard, we will never (without doing real damage) measure up! That's why we have third graders on diets and an epidemic of eating disorders.

All of us have an ideal image we strive for. This is the person we want to look like and be. We also have a current reality. This is who we are and how we look right now. The difference between our ideal and our reality should be called *an action plan*. It is what we do to move closer to the ideal.

Too often we don't bridge the gap with positive, empowering action. We fill the gap with destructive behaviors and messages. We treat the person we are with contempt because that person has failed to achieve the ideal. The contempt is exaggerated when the ideal is ridiculous and unrealistic. We end up hating who we are because of something we literally cannot be!

Self-esteem is not something you get and keep forever. It is something you must work to build and maintain. It's critical that you do, because your children will inherit your self-esteem, and your child's self-esteem is the foundation for the choices she will make throughout life.

Children with a high, healthy self-esteem are optimistic about life and its possibilities. They handle difficult situations, bounce back from adversity, resist negative pressures, and deal with conflict. These children laugh more, reach beyond themselves, and relate well to others! This is what parents want for their children—to enjoy life and make the most of every opportunity!

The problems that accompany low self-esteem are frightening for a parent. Children with low self-esteem are fearful, reluctant to try new things, critical of themselves and others, negative, passive, and ill equipped to handle conflict and challenge. Children with low self-esteem develop negative coping strategies and self-destructive behaviors.

This is by far one of the most important parenting assignments you will ever receive—to develop strong self-esteem in your child—equipping your child to maximize the opportunities and meet the challenges of life.[7]

Knowing we need to develop a strong self-concept is one thing. Knowing how to do that is another. Here are thirteen actions you can take right now to build your self-esteem and develop positive expectancy.

1. *Identify and replace your self-limiting beliefs.* This is where we began, and it continues to be an important theme in cultivating hope. You will never rise above what you believe about yourself.

2. *Teach people how to treat you.* We do indeed teach others how to treat us by what we accept and the boundaries we establish. Is there anyone in your life right now who needs retraining? In a later chapter you will discover why boundaries are so important to relationships and how to set productive boundaries in your personal and professional life.

3. *Learn something new.* Be a lifelong learner. Add skills and capabilities to your personal toolbox. You'll not only become more confident, but you'll also be more competent.

4. *Listen to and read positive, motivating messages.*
Undoubtedly you have heard the saying, "Garbage in, garbage out." Fiercely guard what climbs into your brain! Turn your car into a rolling university! Listen to motivating speakers and authors. Read about successful lives and breakthrough strategies. Study successful people and know that what is possible for them is also possible for you. I dare you to try this for a week! You will be amazed at the difference in your outlook and output.

5. *Remove "I should have" from your vocabulary.*
Perhaps you should or could have done things differently. You didn't, so here you are. *Should haves* change nothing. Say instead, "What I learned is…" or "What I will do differently in the future is…"

6. *Use positive affirmations.* The messages we receive from the *outside* can be very negative and cynical. We must be very good at managing our messages from the inside out. This includes how we talk about ourselves and to ourselves. In pages to come you'll discover the power of the blessing and how to apply it to your life.

7. *Step out of your comfort zone and take a risk.* Confident people take risks and try new things. They aren't afraid of looking foolish or making a mistake. People with less confidence tend to play it safe. I encourage you to step out of your comfort zone, try something new, allow yourself to look foolish for a moment, and find out that is not fatal.

8. *Document your successes.* This is the kind of documentation I heartily recommend! Create a victory file

and use it to track your results and accomplishments. When you receive a note of thanks or recognition from a colleague, place it in the file! (By the way, this is a wonderful tool for performance appraisals. Next time your boss asks what have you accomplished this year, you won't be thinking, "I know I did some stuff, but I just can't remember what it was." You will be able to confidently discuss your achievements.) Your victory file is also a great strategy when you feel your confidence withering. Pull out the file and replay your successes.

9. *Have a victory meeting with your team or family.* (This is one of the most popular tips I offer in conferences. Managers and employees love it. People take this discipline home to their families. The feedback is fabulous, and it costs nothing to implement.) A victory meeting is simply a huddle at the end of the week to highlight the wins. Every person comes to the meeting prepared to talk about a victory they have experienced throughout the week. The key is to celebrate what is right and what is working. (Let's face it; people are people. No matter how much you admire or even love someone, if you are around them long enough, eventually they will irritate you.) Over time we may actually focus more on what isn't working and what people *aren't*. The victory meeting works because it reminds us of what people *are* and what they are trying to become. It recalibrates our focus and gives us positive momentum. It also allows us to recognize and support progress. (I really, really want you to try this ten-minute attitude makeover.)

10. *Help someone else.* Ironically, one of the best ways to build your own self-esteem is to focus on others. There is something in that connection—in the process of forgetting myself and focusing on another human being. It builds my own confidence and self-regard. I am also putting into play a promise of God: "Remember this—a farmer who plants only a few seeds will get a small crop. But the one who plants generously will get a generous crop" (2 Cor. 9:6).

11. *Build a solid network of support.* I'm pretty passionate about networking—especially for women. In my book *Designed for Success*, I asked the question, "Will your net hold?"[8] With a strong network of support, we can take more risk, accept greater challenges, and navigate difficult situations with more confidence. Build your network and watch your confidence grow.

12. *Set and work toward challenging goals.* This is a conscious decision to design the life you want! As you achieve your goals, your confidence soars. As you gain confidence, you can imagine even greater possibilities. We will discuss goal setting in chapter 12, "Making It Real." For now, begin to think about what you want to have, do, and be.

13. *Reward yourself.* As you set goals, build in meaningful rewards. How will you celebrate these accomplishments? These celebrations are mile markers on your journey; they honor and validate your progress.

## JOURNALING EXERCISE

This is a good place to stop and review your list of self-limiting beliefs. The process of exchanging those for empowering beliefs is more than reflection and analysis. We don't think and hope and wish for more empowering beliefs; self-esteem is not something we *have*—it is what we experience when we *do*.

1. What are you learning about yourself as you review your lists?

2. What actions will you take to grow your list of empowering beliefs?

3. If your children were to inherit your current *sense of self*, would they be receiving a treasure? What do you want to change about the inheritance they are receiving?

# 6

# BREAK THE WORRY HABIT

*Worry is the great stumbling block of the mind*

WHEN I ASK THE people in any audience, "Do you worry?" the response is a nearly unanimous, "Yes!" Many admit to having a *master's degree* in worry. They have perfected the art of worrying with a lifetime of practice. And in all of the worry, nothing of real value is gained.

Worry will never change an outcome, solve a problem, or invite a miracle. Creativity will. Persistence will. Action will. Prayer will. But worry cannot. In fact, worry will keep you from doing all of the things that will make a difference.

We have received such good counsel concerning worry: "Who of you by worrying can add a single hour to his life?" (Matt. 6:27, NIV). The King James Version translates the verse: "...can add one cubit unto his stature?" What we focus on we feed, and what we feed grows. When we feed our problems with worry, they will grow. Our problems then become like giants, and in comparison, we feel small and vulnerable.

From author and speaker Brian Tracy I have learned that worry is actually goal setting in reverse. In *The Psychology of Achievement*, Tracy warns that: "We are traveling in the direction of our most dominant thought."[1] In other words, you are heading for what you are thinking about. Just imagine throwing your car into reverse, slamming your foot on the gas pedal, and trying not to bang into something. That is a good analogy for worry.

Tracy's theory resonated with me, and then I had the opportunity to learn it in a very physical way.

My family lived in Minneapolis for a short time. We discovered almost immediately that Minneapolis is the birthplace of the Rollerblade. Our home was on a parkway with miles of biking, running, and Rollerblading paths. I loved to sit on the front steps of my home and watch people glide by on their blades. It looked effortless; they were graceful like gazelles. Some of them would nonchalantly turn and sail by backward! Waving and smiling and flying backward!

That's when I decided to join the ranks of the Rollerblading public.

When I announced this to my son, who was, at that time, in the fifth grade, he was wholeheartedly onboard. Off we went to buy our equipment.

I was terribly proud of myself at this moment because I was facing a lifelong personal fear—the fear of falling! (I am not fond of escalators or moving walkways. The thought of skiing—strapping waxed sticks on my feet and rushing down a steep mountain—is unthinkable!) But today I was facing all of those silly fears and taking a risk. I was stepping out of my comfort zone and modeling effective behaviors for my child. (I probably should have been nominated for some kind of mothering award.)

Tabor had his blades on before mine were even out of the box, and he was off like a bullet down the parkway, whooping it up and yelling for me to, "Come on!" I was amazed at how quickly he took to it. We had never done this before, and he was already flying around like he'd been born on wheels. I remember thinking, "My goodness, these are magic shoes! No wonder it looks effortless."

Finally I was ready, and I gingerly hobbled out to the parkway. I was terrified of going too fast and wiping out. The parkway suddenly looked steep and dangerous. Within fifteen minutes the ambulance arrived. (Don't get sucked into the Rollerblading illusion! You can really, really hurt yourself on those horrible things.)

In the emergency room, I was bitter. "I don't get it," I snapped at my child. "You put them on for the first time and have a wonderful ride. I put them on and 911 is on the line."

His answer was profound (irritating, but profound). In his classic, matter-of-fact way he replied, "All I was thinking about was going faster, and all you were thinking about was falling down. I guess we both ended up where we thought we would be." (I resisted an incredible urge to clobber him. So much for the mothering award.)

*We are headed for what we are thinking about. That's why we get what we are afraid of and not what we want.*

Time and again I find that worry and fear cannot live in the same space with hope and action. They are enemies and cannot survive in the same room. One will always drive out the other. When you stand on faith and take positive action, you evict worry and fear. When you allow fear and worry to move in, hope and action are driven away.

Sometimes worry is in the front of the mind—a problem or situation you are intensely focused on. Other times, it is like the background noise in an elevator—you aren't really listening to it, but it is always there. This kind of worry is vague apprehension or generalized uneasiness. It is hard to put your finger on it, as it slowly drains you. It's like leaving a dome light on in your car. Slowly the battery dies, and the car won't start.

The first step in breaking the worry habit is to become more aware of when you are worrying and what you are worrying about. Catch yourself in the act of doing it! Don't allow worry or fear to play in some corner of your mind, just beyond your reach. Pull it out into the light and squarely face it.

I actually encourage you to make a worry list. Go ahead; indulge yourself! Take a moment now to write down every single worry that is causing you emotional distress, anxiety, or fear.

Once you have completed your list, cross off anything you cannot personally control or impact. (You may find your list is considerably shorter or *gone*.) This is an important revelation. It means you are giving a lot of your mental, physical, and emotional energy to things you cannot affect. And when you are worrying about what you can't impact, you aren't focusing on what you can. You are giving your strength away! You are draining your battery.

The moment we focus on the action we can take, the decision we can make—what we can do, a critical shift occurs. We move from a state of worry into a state of action. And action, you will find, is a marvelous cure for worry.

Candice is a hardworking, single mother of two, holding on by financial threads. The bills are piling up, and the ends don't meet. The knot in her stomach grows every time she reaches into the mailbox for the late notices or when the phone rings with another collection call. Worry is her constant companion. To cope, she leaves the mail unopened and doesn't pick up the phone. She is isolated, perpetually exhausted, and has lost interest in things that used to give her great joy.

Candice is a cycle of worry, denial, and avoidance. By trying to ignore the problem, she exacerbates it. She is giving her strength to the fear, and it is paralyzing her. Each passing day, the problem grows, and she falls further behind. I guarantee this is having an impact on her work, her health, her self-esteem, and her ability to care for her children.

To make the shift, Candice must take back the reins of her financial life. She must develop a plan and take action. This may begin as baby steps and grow (with her confidence and understanding) into a plan for financial freedom and even wealth creation.

There are dozens of things Candice can *do* to empower herself and change her financial course. She will need to educate and discipline herself, and it will require courage, hard work, and faith. But she won't do any of that until she begins to focus on the pieces she can personally impact. Worry will not change the course; it will take her deeper and deeper into a maze of despair.

Return now to your list of worries and pick one. Because you've been worrying about it, you probably have a pretty clear image of what you *don't* want—the worst-case scenario. I'll bet you can describe in great detail what you are afraid could happen. Let's flip that over.

How do you want this situation to turn out? What is the *best-case scenario?* This may be a little harder, because you haven't been practicing for this outcome!

In the case of Candice, she has been mentally rehearsing financial disaster for months. At first it may feel awkward and even unrealistic for her to imagine herself financially in control—debt-free, saving money, and providing easily for her children.

To break the habit of excessive worry, you may even want to make an appointment with worry. This may sound ridiculous, but it is actually very effective. Instead of allowing worry to follow you around everywhere, set aside a specific time and place for it. When you catch yourself worrying outside of the appointment, simply stop and remind yourself, "I will think about this at my worry appointment."

Keep your appointments with worry by writing down what is weighing on your mind, isolating the pieces you can impact, imagining the outcome you want, and identifying the steps you can take to get there. Your appointments with worry will soon become appointments with action, and you will begin to see the most remarkable results.

## WHICH REPORT WILL YOU BELIEVE?

As the children of Israel prepared to enter the Promised Land, twelve spies were sent ahead to explore the land and bring back a report. After forty days, they returned. Ten of the scouts spread discouragement and fear through the community. "The land we traveled through and explored will devour anyone who goes to live there. All the people we saw were huge" (Num. 13:32). This report created such despair! The people wailed and wept and pouted in their tents. They forgot the great miracles they had seen with their own eyes, and they lost sight of the promises before them.

Only two of the men who explored the land (Joshua and Caleb) brought back an encouraging report. "The land we traveled through and explored is a wonderful land! And if the LORD is pleased with us, he will bring us safely into that land and give it to us" (Num. 14:7–8).

There are two questions I would ask of you now.

1. *Which report will you believe?* Will you believe the report that inspires fear and discouragement, or the one that encourages you to step into your *land of promise?*

2. *Which report do you bring to others?* Are you among the ten who spread despair and fear, or the two who strengthen the heart and prepare people to step confidently into their destiny?

There is a special place in my heart for Caleb, who brought the report of hope and encouragement. I count it an honor to be the *Caleb* in someone's life. The report is good! Your promises are waiting for you, and you will be successful!

Here are five more high-impact ideas for breaking the worry habit:

1. *Read about and study great turnarounds*—these are stories of people, communities, teams, and organizations that made great comebacks. You will find inspiring examples of faith, hope, persistence, and action.

2. *Surround yourself with hopeful people*—people who have a relentless faith, people who see the possibility and the promise, and remove yourself from those who are pessimistic and negative. When you do this, the

crowd will clear. There are fewer Joshuas and Calebs around, and the world is full of spies with frightening reports.

3. *Begin each day with positive affirmations*—about your life, your goals, and your possibilities.

4. *Take the advice of Dale Carnegie*—the perfect way to conquer worry is prayer.[2]

5. *Come to the end of yourself*—the weight of worry you are carrying is too heavy. When you get to the end of you, God will take it from there. He will not take it away from you—you must hand it over! Then He will do what you cannot (and He'll make it look easy).

## JOURNALING EXERCISE

At your next appointment with worry, do the following to regain your focus and your positive momentum.

1. Make a list of your worries.
2. Choose one worry and write a detailed description of what you are hoping will happen in this situation.
3. With the positive outcome in mind, list the steps you can take to move in that direction.

# 7

# BOUQUET OF THORNS

*Releasing the offenses that poison*

I**T HAS BEEN SAID,** "Resentment is like drinking poison and waiting for the other person to die." With what we now know about deadly emotions, that is absolutely true! A compelling body of research confirms the direct connection between what we feel as emotions and how we feel physically.[1]

The offenses we carry *are* deadly toxins, and they are heavy. These are the things people have done or have not done, said or did not say. They are the betrayals, broken trusts, and slights. Some wounds are more insidious; they are purposeful, spiteful actions loaded with hurt, aimed right at us.

Sometimes people hurt us intentionally; at other times they did not mean to do us harm. In both cases we hurt, and while the circumstances bringing offenses to bear may be different, all of them have something in common: they are heavy to carry.

To illustrate just how heavy, I'll use a story.

A woman has a longstanding appointment with her therapist. Each week she arrives carrying the weight of the world on her shoulders. She literally stoops under a burden of care. Every week she counts and recounts her wounds. One by one she pulls them out to look at them, talk about them, and relive them.

Her story really is a tragedy. She has been profoundly wounded, and she didn't deserve to be. These are not trivial matters. They are literally heartbreaking.

On this particular day, the woman arrives as expected. She seats herself across from the therapist and draws a breath to begin. He listens patiently as she details the causes of her pain. As she mentions each offense, he places a stone into a backpack on the table between them. She finds this odd, but he says nothing, so she continues. With each offense, a stone is silently placed into the pack. This continues for the entire appointment. She counts the hurts; he places stones into the bag. When her time is over, she rises to leave.

As she reaches the door, he stops her. He secures the pack squarely upon her shoulders and tells her, "These are your wounds. I want you to carry them with you constantly until I see you again. Do not put them down. Keep them with you at all times."

The following week at the appointed time the woman returns. She drags herself into the office and drops the pack of stones at the feet of her therapist. "I cannot carry this any longer. It is too heavy! I can't function like this, and I won't carry these rocks out of here."

The therapist smiled, took a stone out of the bag, and said, "Good. Your decision not to carry this burden any longer is what I've been waiting for. Now we can begin."

This story illustrates in part why it is so important to forgive. Let's be real here; sometimes we won't feel like forgiving. We will feel like striking back. ("I will forgive you only after you have been punished appropriately.")

Forgiving is first a decision—a choice. That's pretty simple. I have been hurt, and I am choosing to forgive. From there it becomes more complicated. How do I forgive the person who has wounded me, whether purposefully or not? Even if I want to, how do I go from the hurt, through the anger (and the need for my justice), to the healing?

More than once in my life I have valiantly declared, "I have forgiven," only to find months or even years later that the wound was not healed. I had simply pushed the pain into the closet of my heart. Without warning, the closet door flew open, and everything stuffed inside came spilling out. I could feel the pain as strongly as the day the offense happened.

Even though I had decided to forgive, I had not completed the work. There is first a decision and then a process. If you stop with the decision to forgive, the work is not done. The forgiveness you've declared is unfinished business, and you will be back to work through the process in the future. (This is one of those "lessons not learned shall be repeated" scenarios.)

There will be many hurts in life, but they are not created equally. If someone cuts me off on the freeway, I may be annoyed. (Scratch that. I will be annoyed.) If someone with thirty-five items (and yes, I have been known to count them) stands in the "10 Items or Less Line" in the grocery store and GETS AWAY WITH THAT, I will be irritated. But as Lewis B. Smedes teaches in his book *Forgive and Forget: Healing the Hurts We Don't Deserve*, some things don't need forgiving—they just need patience, perspective, and a good sense of humor.[2]

We must be careful what we give our strength to. Honestly, there are many situations that are simply not worthy of your attention or your strength. (We only have so much strength to go around, so we need to be pretty selective.)

Other wounds cut deeper. They aren't mild annoyances or petty issues. Smedes writes about these too. "The hurt that creates a crisis of forgiving has three dimensions. It is always personal, unfair, and deep. When you feel this kind of three-dimensional pain, you have a wound that can be healed only by forgiving the one who wounded you."[3]

Forgiveness isn't the noble and righteous thing to do when someone hurts us deeply. It is what we do to heal. And until we do, the wound will impact our lives in ways we may not even recognize.

I love the story about a king who was an avid hunter. For years he hunted with a loyal and skilled guide. Together they would go deep into dangerous jungles. One day, the king's gun misfired, and he lost a thumb. He was very angry and blamed his faithful friend. In a rage, he threw this longtime companion into prison.

Months pass, and the king continued to hunt. One terrible day, he was hunting alone (because his faithful guide and friend was in prison) and found himself surrounded by cannibals. They captured him—his fate was certain. Then suddenly the cannibals set him free. (Apparently it is not a good thing to eat anyone who is missing anything, like a thumb.)

The ruler rushed back to the prison and freed his loyal friend. He begged forgiveness of his friend: "How can you ever forgive me for throwing you into this dark dungeon for so long? Losing my thumb actually saved me! You saved my life months ago, and I didn't see that until now."

The friend softly replied, "I do forgive you, my king. Actually, it might have been worse. If I had not been here in prison, I would have been with you in the jungle, and I have both of my thumbs."

What a marvelous perspective! This story reminds us that forgiveness always unlocks more than one door. When I forgive, I let go of my need for retribution and my *right* to punish you. I release you from an *emotional* prison, and in that moment I set myself free as well. I am free of bitterness and the need for vengeance. I unlock two doors—yours and mine.

This is true even when we are *right*. Imagine for a moment you are driving and approaching an intersection; your light is green. From the corner of your eye you see a car speeding toward the intersection. This car should stop, but it doesn't appear to be slowing down. You say to yourself, "I have the green light! I have the right of way. It's my turn!" With that you punch the gas.

That's when your car crashes into the other vehicle. As author Bill Ligon illustrates with this story, you can be 100 percent right, but if you allow bitterness into your life, there will be a collision, and there will be damage to both vehicles![4]

There are two paths available to us when we have been wounded by another person. Inherently that means we choose to heal or to allow the wound to infect the way we think, feel, and act in the future.[5] When we are hurt, the natural response may be to detach—to withdraw emotionally. Withdrawal is a form of punishment, and it will not solve the problem. Detachment does not invite resolution. Even worse, it is the first step down a very destructive path.

Sometimes we punish people passively. It's not what I say that will get you; it's what I don't say. It's not what I do; it's what I won't do. I withdraw emotionally (also known as pouting) because you've been very, very bad, and you haven't been punished nearly enough.

When I withdraw emotionally, you may spin into performance mode. You may not even understand what you did wrong, but you're going to make it up to me. You'll work extra hard to gain my approval. This is pure manipulation—a form of emotional control. I control you with my hurt. Forgiveness is a real problem for me, because if I forgive you, I don't control you. Forgiveness snips the strings from the puppet, and I can no longer make you dance.

The choices we make when we are hurt by others become the seeds we plant. These seeds don't just grow in one area of our life or in one relationship. They don't stay where we plant them! That is the counsel of the scripture: "Keep a sharp eye out for weeds of bitter discontent. A thistle or two gone to seed can ruin a whole garden in no time" (Heb. 12:15, THE MESSAGE).

My parents still live in a beautiful town in Eastern Oregon where I grew up. Several years ago my mother called to tell me about a gardening mystery in lovely Baker City. The owners of a funeral home had planted tulip bulbs in the fall (fully expecting tulips to arrive in the spring). The tulips did appear—just not where they had been planted!

When spring arrived, dozens of tulips began popping up all over the grounds; the tulips were blooming everywhere except where they had been planted! The mystery was solved by my mother. She had seen where the tulips were planted. But she had also noticed the squirrel that tirelessly labored to dig up and move each one. Things don't always stay where we plant them; they pop up in other places as well.

This *gardening mystery* happens in our lives and relationships too. What we *plant* in one relationship will spread (above and below the surface) to impact all of our relationships. It is true of what we purposefully plant, and it is also true of weeds.

Have you noticed weeds can grow anywhere overnight? We don't intend to plant weeds, but we do water and feed them and nurture them in a dozen ways. As they grow, they choke the life out of what is beautiful. Over time the weeds thrive, and the flowers die. What a paradox!

A woman once told me she had wasted *the best years of her life* in a failed marriage. She went on to tell me how she had once been beautiful and full of life. Her marriage had taken that from her—it had taken everything and given nothing in return. As gently as possible I disagreed. "Your marriage did not steal your youth or your beauty. You traded those things for bitterness. Nothing has been taken from you. You authorized the exchange."

Please understand there is not one ounce of judgment or condemnation in those words. I understand she is hurt and disappointed, and with each passing day this woman is trading her life for her bitterness! It is the story she tells about her past, but like a weed it is consuming her future. Thankfully, her story does not end there.

She has learned that forgiveness is not an event or an emotion. It is a process and a decision. She has also learned that forgiveness is something she controls. It is not dependent on a response from the person who hurt her. She realizes that forgiveness doesn't necessarily equal reconciliation with another person. (And it certainly doesn't mean that we go back for more hurt.) She is learning to pull the roots of bitterness and resentment from her life using steps like these:

1. *Count the cost.* What is the bitterness costing you? How is it impacting the quality of your life? How is this event popping up and creeping into your future? How is it poisoning the soil of your heart? When you

take time to count the cost, you will find yourself
ready to drop this bag of rocks!

2. *Acknowledge what has been lost.* Forgiveness is not a
   mask we slap on to cover what hurts. Acknowledging
   the pain is part of the healing process. Give yourself
   permission to grieve.

3. *Confront the offense.* This does not necessarily mean
   confront the *offender.* In fact, that is often irrelevant
   and counterproductive. It is the offense, not the
   person, that you need to confront. This is where you
   face what happened, how you felt, and how it has
   impacted you. This may be a conversation you have, or
   it may be a personal, reflective exercise.

4. *Own your piece of the action.* What was your contri-
   bution to this situation? How did you participate in the
   offense? This is not about blaming yourself; it is taking
   your power back. You are not a victim.

5. *Decide to forgive.* Again, this is a decision, not an
   emotion. Even as you decide to forgive, you may be
   deeply hurt. That is the paradox. Forgiveness is the
   prescription for the pain. If you wait until you feel
   like forgiving, the seeds of bitterness may have already
   taken hold.

6. *Plug into the right resources.* This is not the time to
   surround yourself with people who will identify with
   your pain and support your right to keep it. Connect
   with people (even professionals) who will help you
   release the hurt and move through the process.

7. *Pray.* Authentic forgiveness is not something we can conjure up. It is something we must reach for and diligently seek. This is the kind of prayer that moves the heart of God.

Unfortunately, there are people who will not take these steps. They will continue to wear bitterness and disappointment like a badge. It is their *hall pass* in life, excusing them from productive behaviors and attitudes. If we don't manage the hurts and disappointments in our lives, we risk becoming the toxic people others are trying to pull from theirs!

## JOURNALING EXERCISE

1. Where have you stopped with the decision to forgive without going through the process of forgiveness?

2. What offenses are *popping up* in other places of your life?

3. What must you *give up* to forgive your offenders?

# 8

# TOXIC ALLIANCES

*Pulling relationships that hinder your growth*

I N TERMS OF PURE definition, an *alliance* is an agreement, part-
nership, or connection. Stand those words next to *toxic*, and you
have a dangerous alliance, a poisonous connection, or a deadly
agreement. That understanding alone should be motivation enough
to pull toxic influences from your life!

What this really means is that sometimes we must *pull* people
from our lives. I do not say that flippantly. It can be difficult and
painful to end a relationship. What is even worse is allowing a
relationship—even a long-term one—to derail you, incapacitate you,
or steal your credibility and your joy.

While we may not purposefully align or partner with toxic people,
we do that when we passively accept or participate in their behavior.
When we don't remove ourselves from the situation or confront the
behavior, we endorse it by default. (This can be one of those "it's not
what you say or do; it's what you don't say or do" scenarios.)

When you get right down to it, there are basically two groups of
people in the world. In the first group are people who encourage and
believe in you. They add something to you. When you leave their
presence you feel better. You are more confident, more prepared, and
equipped. These people export hope!

The second group I call *vampire people*, because they suck the
life out of everything and everyone they touch! You can almost hear
the giant vacuum fire up when they walk into a room. These people
are absolutely miserable, they love company, and they are constantly

recruiting members. (By the way, membership is not free. It will cost you more than you can imagine.)

In the workplace, toxic alliances are co-workers who constantly draw others into negative conversations. They are the ones who want to argue incessantly and debate trivial points. (They swat at gnats while elephants stomp all over them.) These people draw energy (and attention) from gossip, criticism, arguing, and whining. They terrorize meetings, projects, and teams. They aren't just connected to the rumor mill—they manage it!

You know the type; they are famous for throwing rocks to get everyone stirred up, innocently hiding their hands and standing back to watch the show. (At this point, faces and names may be flashing before your eyes!)

In our personal and professional lives, toxic people are colleagues, friends, and family members who criticize, attack, and divide. They are often masters of *the dig*. They don't really come right out and say things; they insinuate them and leave you wondering, "What did that mean?" They use sarcasm like a precision tool to push your buttons and enjoy holding up your weaknesses for the world to see. They twist the truth with amazing skill until it is unrecognizable. Quite often, toxic behavior crosses the line of integrity and becomes unethical behavior.

We don't pick our family, right? That is probably true for co-workers and colleagues as well. We don't always get to choose whom we work with or for. We do control how we interact with the people in our personal and professional lives. We control our boundaries and our *scripts*. We control access to our hot buttons!

Ask yourself these questions to see if you have a toxic relationship poisoning the soil of your heart:

1. Is there anyone planting negative, critical beliefs into your life right now? When you are with this person, how do you feel?

2. Is there a relationship in your life that is pulling you backward, blocking your growth, and undermining your progress? What is that costing you?

3. Is there a relationship marked by broken trust, unresolved conflict, and destructive communication? How much of your strength are you giving to this?

4. Is there someone in your life who compromises your boundaries or ethics? What impact is that having?

5. Are there behaviors you are passively endorsing to avoid conflict? What do you risk with your silence?

Questions like these allow you to step back and assess the situation. At the same time, you will want to consider your role. How are you enabling or perpetuating the toxic pattern? And if you really want to do some soul searching, ask yourself this tough question: What is the payoff? What do you gain from this toxic relationship? (Or what will you give up if the situation improves?) You may be surprised by your answers here.

Sometimes we hold on to a toxic situation because we get something from it. For example, we get to feel superior, or we get our grievances validated. If you find a payoff in your toxic situation, you must be willing to give that up before you can move forward in an authentic way.

Loyalty also connects us to toxic people. We don't want to abandon or hurt them, so we stay. We continue to give them our strength, but they don't get stronger—we get weaker. The relationship is very one-sided—one person gives and another takes. This is also called codependency. It isn't healthy for either person.

It is absolutely essential to guard your focus with toxic people. Otherwise you will go around in circles until you are dizzy and sick to your stomach. Your communications with them must be objectives-based.

That means you don't engage at their level. You keep your eye on a worthy objective, like a bulldog with a bone.

Perhaps one of the greatest mistakes we make (and one of the ways we take our eyes off the objective) with toxic people is trying to understand them and figure out why they do what they do. Like amateur psychologists, we attempt to diagnose the dysfunction. Here's a public service announcement for you: "It's not your problem!" Even in trying to understand them we get sucked into their weird dysfunction. That is the plan! Even when they aren't in the room, they are the center of attention, and this pleases them very much.

---

## Public Service Announcement:
## It's not your problem!

---

I was amazed as I watched a team of people in a large organization working through a tough technical problem. For the most part, this was a dedicated group of people who were onboard and focused on finding a solution together—except for one.

This team member turned every topic into a debate and took the opposite position on every point. At first I was embarrassed for her; then I realized she was having a marvelous time! This is how she gets her attention. She was performing on a stage of her own making. Every eye in the room was on her. (Most of them were rolling, but still they were on her.) Everyone was trying to help her understand, working to get her agreement, and addressing her issues. Incidentally, this wasn't because they cared about her feelings or found real merit in her objections; they just wanted to move on!

After the meeting she proudly told me, "I like to play the devil's advocate. It keeps the group on their toes." With that she turned and marched off to dismantle another project. In her wake, she left a group of frustrated people who had just allowed an hour of time to be wasted. They spent the next ten minutes discussing her, so the clock didn't actually stop when she left the room. (I think she would have been pleased about that as well.)

Bev dreads the holidays because it means interacting with what she refers to as "the most dysfunctional family on the planet." At these gatherings, toxic behavior abounds. There is plenty of criticism, comparison, and condescension to go around. As Bev puts it, "Before I hang up my coat, I am feeling defensive. These events are real self-esteem busters. My family can knock the confidence out of anyone, but it's usually me. I am always reminded of my perfect sister who has married the perfect man and created three perfect children."

Both of these scenarios are frustrating and realistic examples of toxic behavior. What may be missing in these situations are ground rules. The players haven't established rules to protect the relationships or the results. Unacceptable behaviors aren't confronted, so frustration grows along with the dysfunction.

## HAVE YOUR SCRIPTS READY

The first time toxic behavior takes me off guard and I don't know how to respond, that's probably fair. If it spins me around a second time, I own that. This is when a good *script* comes in handy, and you'll want to prepare in advance, because toxic people will be back. Here are three scripts most of us can use at some point in our lives to confront toxic behavior:

1. Do you have anyone in your life who has perfected what I call *the drive-by jab*? This person doesn't really tell you what's on her mind; she carefully wraps the dig in sarcasm or an *ever-so-innocent* comment. The next time she *drives by* with one of her innuendos, look her directly in the eye, smile warmly, and say, "I think I hear some feedback in there somewhere. Is there something you're trying to tell me?" (She will

immediately fold and declare her innocence. Of course she didn't mean anything by it! She was just joking. But I guarantee that she'll think twice before driving by again.)

2. What about the co-worker who brings you the latest gossip about another colleague? You are not comfortable with this information, but you don't know what to say. Try this: "I would feel horrible if someone said that about me." (Expect a stunned silence here. And if your co-worker has any sense, it will be a stunned and embarrassed silence! She probably won't be bringing you her news bulletins in the future.)

3. Then there are people who infect everyone with their negativity. The next time they are whining and complaining, ask a solution-oriented question like: "What can you do to make this better?" or "What pieces of this problem do you control?" (Again there will be silence, because you are asking for solutions, and they don't have any of those handy.)

In each of these scenarios, you are essentially teaching people how to treat you. You are setting boundaries and laying ground rules. Firmly and gracefully you are sending a message: "Knock it off! Don't go there with me." The key is preparation. If you are dealing with a toxic person, write your script in advance.

This is a little like shock therapy for toxic people, so you'll have to be patient in the process. You may have to repeat the lesson more than once, so stand your ground. Eventually they will get it. They will either snap out of the toxic pattern or move along to someone who doesn't have a good script. (You win either way.)

There may come a time in your life when you must decide to

completely disengage from a toxic person—to end a relationship. It's helpful to remember you aren't moving them. *You are moving you.* You are making a healthy choice for your life.

Sometimes nothing needs to be said in situations like this. You go your way, and that takes care of it. If only it were always that easy! In the case of long-term relationships or even family members, it probably won't be as simple as just moving on.

Remember Bev with the perfect sister? The family gatherings became so unhealthy for her that she could no longer accept the behavior by participating. For two years she successfully avoided family events with a thousand lame excuses. This may have excused her from the table, but it did nothing to solve the problem. Eventually she did muster up the courage to tell her mother the truth. "It was agonizing, but when I finally said it…when I actually told her how I felt, it was such a relief! A huge weight lifted, and I felt stronger," Bev recalls. "I used a script, and it gave me confidence to confront the behaviors that were alienating me from my family."

Bev used a format that first described what was happening and what she felt. She then asked for a change in behavior. She asked to be treated differently in the future. Her script ended by stating a desire to participate in family gatherings if the interaction became healthier. When you put those pieces together, it sounded like this:

> When we are together as a family, I am constantly being compared to my sister and falling short of the mark. This hurts, and it is damaging my relationship with her and with you. I need the comparisons and the competition to stop. I love this family, and I want to participate in our gatherings. I can only do that if we can learn how to respect and encourage each other. If that's not possible, I must decline future invitations.

Notice the "I" messages in this script. Bev took complete responsibility for what she felt and what she was asking for. She did not assign blame by saying, "You compare me, you hurt me, or you need to stop treating me this way." She also asked for what she wanted; she asked for a change in behavior. That is the key that will unlock a new pattern of interaction.

It was a little awkward at first. Bev admits, "We had some well-established patterns of communication. We had to break out of those." Over time this situation has greatly improved, and Bev looks forward to seeing her family, especially her mother. It's ironic that for years Bev had avoided having this conversation. Ultimately the avoidance was destroying the most important relationships in her life.

Bev has this to say about the energy she added to the dysfunction: "For days before family events I imagined how horrible it was going to be, and for days after I seethed with anger about how horrible it was. I would leave my parent's home huffing and puffing and promising never to return. Not dealing with it was making me toxic!"

With all of this in mind, sometimes the toxic behavior is not our problem. When asked how to handle a toxic person, my first questions are always: "What is the impact on you or your results? How does this behavior get in your way?"

If the answer is, "It doesn't," then my advice is *walk away.* We certainly don't need to go looking for toxic people, and we don't get to appoint ourselves the *behavior police!* We lose credibility and waste a great deal of energy when we involve ourselves in situations that do not concern us.

## When Toxic Behavior Is Really Just Unethical Behavior

As we've seen in the examples above, toxic behaviors can be annoying and distracting, destructive and divisive. They can also be a breach of ethics. Toxic behavior is unethical behavior when it breaks down standards and compromises the integrity of the organization.

Ethics has emerged as one of the most visible and even regulated themes of business. Catastrophic ethical breakdowns have resulted in a call for the highest standards in business. The call has been answered with rigorous oversight and even legislation.

Ethics are the values and the *rules*. Integrity is living by them. In those terms, it may be possible to have excellent ethics and a complete breakdown of integrity. We must actively confront behaviors that do not wholeheartedly support what we value.[1]

Just this morning I received an e-mail from a manager in the Caribbean. Her question was, "How can I confront an immoral issue with a team member without having to fire him? He is young, bright, talented, and an asset to our organization professionally speaking, but there is an issue that does not line up with our standards."

Immoral or unethical behavior will tear at the fabric of excellence and pride; it opens a dangerous door. I often tell leaders, "Your true standard is what you are accepting right now."

*When it comes to unethical or immoral behavior, acceptance is authorization!*

If toxic behavior is unethical behavior, it's important to take action. Make sure rules and standards are in place and communicated. "When employees have no clear picture of the moral or ethical stance of the organization, they tend to operate at the lowest perceived level."[2] We also must ensure that we consistently apply the standards. There cannot be different rules for different players.

It is essential to confront unethical behavior. Below is a six-step communication model that will assist in delivering the message effectively:

1. Use facts to describe the behavior that is questionable or risky. (Avoid using judgmental terms or secondhand knowledge. Stick with the facts as you know them.)

2. Communicate the value or standard that is compromised by this behavior.

3. Explain the impact on results, reputation, and credibility. Why is this behavior unacceptable? What will it cost the organization, the team, and the individual?

4. Ask for a change in behavior. Specifically state what you want this person to stop or start doing.

5. Ask for a commitment.

6. Be prepared to talk about the consequences if the behavior does not change.

As you assess the relationships in your life, decide how to deal with toxic people and build your scripts. Remember, this is not about changing other people. We don't get to do that. The goal is not to change them, judge them, or even teach them a well-deserved lesson. The goal is to manage our responses, protect what we value, and create highly functional relationships.

## JOURNALING EXERCISE

1. How are you unintentionally aligning yourself with toxic people?

2. What scripts do you need to prepare?

3. Are there toxic behaviors you recognize in yourself? If so, what needs to change?

9

# EMBRACING CHANGE

*Endings signal new beginnings*

THE ABILITY TO ADAPT and manage change is an important skill set, personally and professionally. Our initial reactions to change aren't always positive. We want things to get better...only...stay the same! The manager of a large call center tells a story that perfectly illustrates that paradox.

In this call center, all the workstations were exactly the same. Agents were allowed to sit anywhere they pleased, log in to the computer, and go right to work. It had been this way for years. Then a new general manager arrived on the scene with a boatload of new ideas to make things better.

His first idea was to create teams and assign seating. You should have heard the wailing and whining! "This is ridiculous. Now they're even telling us where we have to sit! Do they think we are children?"

Before too long, employees settled down and settled into the new routine. They even decorated their workstations and named their teams. The general manager was extremely successful and was recruited to another position in the company.

His replacement arrived with a new boatload of ideas to make things even better. The first grand scheme was to break up the teams and allow people to sit wherever they like. Oh, the wailing and whining you heard throughout the call center! "They can't do this! This is my seat! This is where all my stuff is. I don't care what anybody says, I'm going to sit here every day."

The same people who were absolutely incensed by the idea of

assigned seating were now furious at the thought of giving up that seat! As I said, people are funny. We like things to stay the same, and we want them to get better. *Better* doesn't happen without change.

To illustrate how people feel about and respond to change, I often use a game. I ask people to choose a partner and stand back to back. Once in position, they are instructed to change something about themselves. It can be anything. Most often I see people removing glasses, jewelry, and even their shoes.

After the changes are complete, I ask them to face their partner and try to detect what has changed. There is much laughter as they search for the change and realize they weren't paying attention!

We repeat this process two more times. By the third round, people are groaning and becoming genuinely agitated by all of this change. (Some people become stomping mad over this exercise.)

What this simple game reveals is profound. Subtly, this is what we can take away from the experience:

1. Most people take things off. Rarely do I see people pick something up or add something. Unconsciously we think about change as *losing* stuff —it subtracts something from us.

2. People immediately want to put things back where they were. The change is uncomfortable, and they cannot wait to reverse it. Like a rubber band that has been stretched, we snap back into place when the tension of the situation diminishes.

3. With the first change, people are caught off guard. They weren't noticing others in the environment. By the third round, they are acutely aware and looking for the slightest change. Increasing our awareness allows us to anticipate and prepare for change.

## WHAT ARE YOU CLINGING TO?

In his book *Managing Transitions,* William Bridges shares an important insight. Inside of every change there is an ending, middle, and beginning. Endings are hard, because when something ends, we must let go. When we let go, we feel a loss. When you think about that, change isn't the hard thing after all. Letting go is. As Bridges writes, "We don't resist change. We resist letting go."[1]

You cannot reach for what is new until you let go of the thing you are clutching so tightly. This is a little like holding on for dear life to a rock ledge, terrified of falling. Within your reach is the rope that will carry you to safety. To grasp that lifeline, you must do two things—you must let go of what you are clinging to, and then you must reach out.

How many of us cling to the crumbling ledge and refuse the line to safety? After reaching for that line and climbing to a higher place, have you ever wondered, "Why did I hold on to that for so long?"

Terri begins her *clutching* story with this bold statement: "I'd been holding on so long to this misery, it had almost become a comfortable companion."

Even though she had a big dream for her life, Terri had (like many of us) settled into a respectable job, working for a boss who appeared to be completely over his head. With that lack of leadership, dysfunction grew like a weed. Blame was the first response to every problem and people spent most of their time documenting what others did or did not do.

As the situation became increasingly worse, Terri held on by a thread. She had always been a top performer, but her results were slipping. People who knew her well would not have recognized her at work. She was defensive, negative, and unmotivated. Her boss had become the enemy, and tension continued to grow.

At some level, awareness was building inside: "It is time to go."

Still she held on. She held on, in fact, for months, until the day she was fired for something ridiculous and petty.

"That," she remembers, "was the best day of my working life. It felt horrible in the moment, but it was the best thing that could have happened. It forced me out of my comfort zone. Who knows how long I would have stayed there, losing myself in that dysfunction and allowing the situation to change me. I had become part of the problem. It was hard to see my options or find the energy to pursue them."

When you find yourself in a no-win situation, it's possible...even likely...that you are being pushed not only to the edge but also to the end of yourself. When you get to that place—the end of you— something wonderful can happen. It is called a new beginning.

Change is hard. It is a struggle. We might view change as an event—with a time and a date stamp on it. In reality, change is not just an event. It is also a process, and we manage it in stages. (Interestingly enough, the stages of change closely resemble the stages of grief. Go figure.)

The change you are facing may be at work or in a relationship. It may have to do with your finances or your health. The change bearing down on you might look like a mountain in your path, but large or small, the process is really the same. Regardless of the circumstances, you can probably relate to this sequence:

1. *Denial*—This is when we say things like, "That can't be true," or "This can't really be happening." In denial we do not recognize the need for change. We may not realize there's a problem, and we certainly aren't ready to confront it! There's an important human dynamic at work here. *People will never confront what they are not ready and willing to do something about.*

2. *Resistance*—Here we push back and say, "I can't do this," or "I *won't* do this." In this stage of change, we probably feel out of control, like something is being forced onto us, and we resent it! Pushing back takes a great deal of energy, so in this stage of change people often feel exhausted, disoriented, and unfocused.

3. *Exploration*—In this stage we begin to see the positives and imagine the possibilities. We say, "Maybe I can," and "This might actually work." A glimmer of hope returns. Perhaps we'll make it after all. We may still be tentative in this stage, but we are regaining a sense of balance.

4. *Commitment*—We've made the turn, and we can actually embrace the change. We can finally say, "I will make the most of this." Even in the case of a very difficult change, we might say, "I would never want to do that again, but I wouldn't change it for the world. As painful as this has been, it's one of the most valuable experiences of my life. I have profited from it."

When I coauthored *Thriving in the Midst of Change,* my goal was to transform what we have known about the *stages of change* into the *milestones of change.*[2] Because change is a journey, milestones mark our progress, memorialize our achievements, and translate the steps of change into tangible, practical goals.

Ironically, the milestones of change don't focus on the change per se. They focus on the actions we can take to move forward. They point our eyes to the pieces we can control and remind us that we are powerful. Ultimately we learn that change does affect us, and we can effect change.

Let's revisit the stages of change—now framed as milestones.

## MILESTONE 1: FOCUS ON FACTS

We may safely shelter ourselves for a time in a state of denial, hoping if we ignore this thing long enough it will turn and go away. It won't. Here is an important change principle: *Inside of change, truth is ultimately more helpful than "good news."* If we can discipline ourselves to focus first on the facts rather than the feelings, we begin to grasp the change in a way that makes sense.

As we confront the reality, it is critical to maintain absolute faith. The ability to do that is a hallmark of greatness.[3] This is the faith that confidently insists, no matter what the facts are, that you will come through. You will overcome the obstacles in your path. You will succeed. Without the element of faith, we simply cannot look reality directly in the eye.

You can reach this first milestone by asking questions and learning everything you can about the change. Make it your goal to understand the change and what is causing the need for it. Look behind what is happening to find the *why*. Challenge your assumptions. What are you assuming about this change? What do you believe about it, and what else could be true?

## MILESTONE 2: EMPOWER YOURSELF AND OTHERS

At this milestone, you turn resistance into empowerment. (And it's important that you do, because if you don't, you can get stuck here for a very long time.) People sometimes look and sound like victims inside of change. That's because they feel victimized! It often feels like something is being done *to me*, with or without my permission.

It is very natural to feel a sense of loss when we let go of *how things were*. Here it is important to make room for the feelings. We must acknowledge the emotions inside of change if we want to make successful transitions.

At the same time, we must hold tightly to the knowledge that we don't always control what happens—but we do always control how we respond. We are 100 percent responsible for our responses. There is a powerful principle at work here. Our response to change will shape the outcome.

There is good reason to turn resistance into empowerment. Resistance is absolutely exhausting. It takes a great deal of energy. It is also a natural reflex.

To demonstrate this, I sometimes ask audience members to stand up, choose a partner, and quickly decide who is A and who is B. The partners face each other, with their hands up, palms facing each other (as if preparing to play the child's game patty-cake). When everyone is in position, I shout to the As: "Push on B! Keep pushing, A! Push hard!"

After a few seconds of this crazy pushing, I ask the As to tell me what B did. The answer is almost always the same. B pushed back. Isn't that interesting? B had no instructions.

The first response when we feel *pushed* by change is to resist by pushing back. This looks like inflexibility, it sounds like negativity, and in the end it doesn't accomplish much.

**How do you resist the temptation to resist?**

Resistance may be the natural response, but it may not be the most effective one. Resistance is like driving seventy-five miles an hour down the freeway with the emergency brake fully engaged! You may be moving, but you are tearing up the car! You can release your internal brake by turning your objections into questions.

When Scumaci and I married, he had been living in Seattle, and I was living in San Antonio. Like the true gentlemen he is, he sold his home in Seattle and moved to his new home in Texas.

I loved this home, *especially* the backyard. That was actually one of the reasons I chose it. The backyard was my retreat. When Scumaci arrived in a whirlwind of Italian intensity, he announced almost immediately, "I'd like to change the backyard. I want to make it into an Italian courtyard."

My first reaction was to push back—hard! Just in time, I remembered my skills. Instead of saying, "Over my dead body," or something along that line, I sweetly asked, "What will that look like?" His was a vision of tile and stone, palm trees gently floating in the breeze, and a gargantuan fountain in the center.

Instead of saying, "That sounds very expensive," I asked, "What do you think this will cost?"

He said, "I'll find out."

I needed to say, "This will not add real value to the house." Instead, I asked, "Is this an investment? Does it make our home worth more?"

He said, "I'll ask."

Finally I asked through ever-so-slightly clenched teeth: "When you tear out a tree that has been there for three hundred years, how long does it take for the palms to grow tall and sway properly?"

He said, "I'll check into that."

For several weeks, strangers paraded through our beautiful backyard, measuring and calculating and offering their services. In the end, my husband decided against the Italian courtyard. (Apparently it costs too much, takes too long, and you never really recover the investment.) When he announced his decision, I looked appropriately disappointed. And I surprised myself a little—I actually was a little disappointed.

If you can turn your objections into questions, conflict becomes conversation. And something else happens. When you ask and really listen, you begin to understand the situation at a deeper level. I found myself becoming genuinely interested in the possibilities of this Italian courtyard.

Incidentally, we celebrated our first anniversary with a fountain. Although not mammoth, it is precious to me. Etched in the stone is my life scripture: "'For I know the plans I have for you,' declares the LORD, 'plans to prosper you and not to harm you, plans to give you hope and a future'" (Jer. 29:11, NIV).

**Acknowledge feelings to reduce resistance.**

To reach the second milestone, we must also acknowledge the feelings inside of the change. To ignore how we, or others, feel is counterproductive. This is not commiserating and endless whimpering; it is simply acknowledging how the change feels.

Leaders sometimes want to jump over this step because it feels like they may be reinforcing negativity. I disagree. Until we effectively acknowledge how the change feels, we will continue to meet with resistance. Here are some examples of acknowledgments that work inside of change:

- "This is a very different approach, and it will take some getting used to."

- "We have been through a great deal of change in a short amount of time."

- "This is hard."

When people are acknowledged, they feel understood. Defensiveness and resistance fall away, because there is no need for them anymore. Acknowledgment doesn't validate negativity inside of change—it validates people.

**Hold on to your voice inside of change.**

Even the most valid concerns lose credibility if they are communicated in a negative or resistant way. If we want to have real impact and to be taken seriously, we can't create the perception (or the reputation) for whining and complaining. Here are some examples of how to present your concerns with credibility so you hold on to your voice inside of change. As you compare these statements, which do you think have more credibility and influence?

| "This is stupid." | "I am struggling to understand the objective here." |
| "This won't work. | "I have some questions and concerns about how this will work." |
| "I don't have time for this." | "I am concerned with the impact this will have on priorities and productivity." |

## MILESTONE 3: EXPLORE THE POSSIBILITIES

At the third milestone, energy returns and creativity kicks in. We search for and begin to find the possibilities inside even the most difficult changes. At this point we are able to see and explore options and set goals. We are no longer resisting the change; we are growing through it. We get real traction and build momentum by marking and celebrating progress.

If the change impacts others, involve them! Ask them for help in generating ideas and creating solutions. It is very hard for people to embrace what they cannot affect. The moment we get people involved, they are vested. Involvement creates a sense of ownership. Ownership gives birth to commitment.

## MILESTONE 4: LEVERAGE THE OPPORTUNITY AND THE LEARNING

The final milestone becomes a memorial marking what we have accomplished and what we have learned. We have successfully navigated the change and added something of value to ourselves. We can look back and see how far we've come on our journey and mark the changes we've made. Like a stone in the river, we have been polished by the rough waters of change, and we are more beautiful for the experience.

The table on the next page summarizes actions you can take to reach each milestone of change.

| The Stage of Change | The Milestone | How to Get There | Change Principles |
|---|---|---|---|
| Denial | Tell yourself the truth. | Focus on the facts, not the initial feelings. Confront reality with faith. Gather information before reaching for conclusions or judging the change. | Inside of change, truth is more important than good news. |
| Resistance | Empower yourself and others. | Acknowledge feelings. Rigorously focus on what you can control. Turn your objections into questions. Identify what you need to be successful. Give and ask for support. | Our responses shape our outcomes. We navigate change more successfully if we focus on what we can control. |
| Exploration | Find possibility. | Think options. Get involved, and involve others who are impacted by the change. Set short-term goals. Make progress visible. | Clear goals help you find the most efficient path. |
| Commitment | Leverage the opportunity and the learning. | Market your results. Celebrate the victories! Take away the lessons. Build memorials. | If we will allow it, even the most difficult changes will add something of value to our lives. |

Change is coming, with or without our permission. Some changes will be thrust upon you, and you will want to throw them back! Remember, change isn't just about losing our stuff. If we allow it to, change adds something to us.

Change is uncomfortable, but if we manage it well—if we are open to the opportunity inside of it—the changes we face will become the victories we celebrate.

## Journaling Exercise

1. What changes are you managing now?
2. With these changes in mind, where do you see yourself in the process?
3. What must you do to reach the next milestone?

## Reflections

## Part I: Seeds of Hope

The list below will help you to internalize the principles from part 1 of this book and will give you direction for the actions you can take to confront the beliefs, behaviors, and relationships that must be uprooted—the stones and stumps that must be removed in order for hope to take root. Remember that clearing is a conscious decision to *take back* the ground you may have given over to self-limiting beliefs, learned helplessness, victim mentalities, and toxic alliances.

## Clearing Your Ground for New Growth

- The results you are getting right now, in every area of your life, reflect what you believe! If you want a new result, you must get a new belief.

- Problems are magnified when you look through glasses of fear.

- An event or experience does not have the power to shape our expectations. It is the way we interpret and process the event. It is how we summarize it, how we tell the story, and what we remember about it. It is what we replay in our brain that ultimately carves the memory into our minds.

- You are not a victim of your past, your present, or your genes. You do have choices and options. You can empower yourself, even in the most difficult situations. In the end, it is not what happens to you—it is how you respond that will become the story of your life.

- In the most devastating circumstances, some people focus on what they cannot do and what they have lost. Others focus on what they can control and what they have. Incredibly, those who lose the most are often the most triumphant. What remains (even in the rubble) is a beautiful, relentless hope for the future.

- Self-esteem is not something you get and keep forever. It is something you must work to build and maintain. It's critical that you do, because your children will inherit your self-esteem, and your child's self-esteem is the foundation for the choices she will make throughout life.

- Worry will never change an outcome, solve a problem, or invite a miracle. Creativity will. Persistence will. Action will. Prayer will. But worry cannot. In fact, worry will keep you from doing all of the things that will make a difference. Worry is the great stumbling block of the mind.

- The moment we focus on the action we can take, the decision we can make—what we can do, a critical shift occurs. We move from a state of worry into a state of action. And action, you will find, is a marvelous cure for worry.

- We must be careful what we give our strength to. Honestly, there are many situations that are simply not worthy of your attention or your strength. (We only have so much strength to go around, so we need to be pretty selective.)

- The choices we make when we are hurt by others become the seeds we plant. These seeds don't just grow in one area of our life or in one relationship. They don't stay where we plant them!

- There may come a time in your life when you must decide to completely disengage from a toxic person—to end a relationship. It's helpful to remember you aren't moving them. You are moving you. You are making a healthy choice for your life.

- As you assess the relationships in your life, decide how to deal with toxic people, and build your scripts. Remember, this is not about changing other people. We don't get to do that. The goal is not to change them, judge them, or even teach them a well-deserved lesson. The goal is to manage our responses, protect what we value, and create highly functional relationships.

- You cannot reach for what is new until you let go of the thing you are clutching so tightly. This is a little like holding on for dear life to a rock ledge, terrified of falling. Within your reach is the rope that will carry you to safety. To grasp that lifeline, you must do two things—you must let go of what you are clinging to, and then you must reach out.

- We don't always control what happens, but we do always control how we respond. We are 100 percent responsible for our responses. There is a powerful principle at work here. Responses ultimately shape outcomes.

- Change is uncomfortable, but if we manage it well—if we are open to the opportunity inside of it—the changes we face will become the victories we celebrate.

*Part II*

# PLANTING

# SOWING SEEDS OF HOPE AND EXPECTANCY

*Some seeds fell on a footpath, and the birds came and ate them. Other seeds fell on shallow soil with underlying rock. The seeds sprouted quickly because the soil was shallow. But the plants soon wilted under the hot sun, and since they didn't have deep roots, they died. Other seeds fell among thorns that grew up and choked out the tender plants.*
—MATTHEW 13:4–7

WHERE DOES HOPE FLOURISH? What are the optimal conditions, and what is the perfect climate for hope to grow? Would it surprise you to learn that the strongest, most vibrant hope can grow vigorously in the most adverse circumstances? The pain you are feeling, the struggle you are in, and the disappointment you have experienced may be seeds of hope and expectancy.

Years ago while living in Colorado, I found an advertisement for a magnificent flower garden in a magazine. It was breathtaking—the perfect mix of color and design, complete with a blueprint for planting. I ordered it immediately with rush delivery, because I could not wait to *install* my new garden.

From the picture, I imagined a large semitruck arriving to deliver my mail-order garden. You cannot imagine my disappointment when the sorry little plantings arrived in one small shoe-sized box. It was pitiful! Nothing but roots and cuttings and strange-looking shoots.

I called my mother immediately to report this cruel gardening scheme! She laughed and said, "Dondi dear, gardens must grow." And the garden did grow. Each year it became more beautiful than the last. Every spring I would wait with such expectancy, watching for the first small signs of what would become nothing short of extraordinary.

## 10

# BOLD BLESSINGS

*Release the power of proclamations*

MUCH HAS BEEN SAID and written about managing one's self-talk and using positive affirmations to develop positive expectancy. I believe in that, but I want to push beyond those concepts and encourage you to do more than say *nice* things to yourself and about yourself. I want you to make bold proclamations for your life, work, and home! I want you to fully release the power of *the blessing* into your life and the lives of those you love.

In biblical times, people deeply understood the power of the blessing. The blessing is permanent and unconditional—spoken with authority. It is not silent! It is a declaration, a proclamation, and a promise. The blessing is used to protect, to promote, and to prosper. I believe in the power of the blessing, and I want that kind of power to operate in my life!

Just as words can build and empower, they are able to cripple and destroy. You must be careful what you say to yourself and others because the words you speak are the seeds you plant in their lives. Whatever is in the seed will grow. It will produce.

It is not nearly enough to stop being negative. I made that mistake for years. I would bite my tongue to keep from saying something negative (and feel very proud of myself when I succeeded). I am learning that is not enough. It is just one-half of the equation. We must replace what is negative and limiting with what is positive and empowering. This is a process in which something must stop (the negativity) and something must start (positive, powerful proclamations).

When it comes right down to it, perhaps we don't really grasp how much power is in the spoken word. We say things lightly and flippantly without realizing the power and permanence in what we speak. In this way words are cheap. But are they really?

What would change if you really believed every word was a seed planted into your life and into the lives of others? What if you knew (without a shadow of doubt) that inside every seed was the awesome potential to produce? And there lies the problem with seeds.

*Seeds can only produce what they are. Seeds of faith produce faith. Seeds of discouragement produce discouragement.*

Let's test that theory. Can you remember something hurtful said to you as a child? I'm betting you can. After all these years, when you think of that situation, can you not feel the sting of the words that were spoken over you? Those words still have the ability to pinch your heart, and they still leave a bruise.

Words do have tremendous power. Once they are released, they keep working. Even your list of empowering and limiting beliefs is evidence of that. The beliefs you have listed were *planted* by your experiences and by words spoken. I encourage you to adopt this simple rule in your life: *Never say anything about yourself or another that you do not sincerely want to be true. Speak life and hope and blessings only.*

Years ago, I was speaking in Southern California. The topic was managing our messages and communicating effectively. In the session, we talked about the power of the spoken word and how we must be so careful not to plant or reinforce what is negative into our own or another's life.

On the break, I stepped outside to enjoy a beautiful day. The first thing I heard was a screeching mother, screaming at her children by the swimming pool: "Don't run. You are going to fall down and break open your face!"

I physically cringed. I wanted to scream back to her, "Are you crazy? Why would you speak something so ugly and dangerous over your children?" (You'll be proud to know that I resisted the temptation and smiled very sweetly.)

Don't say anything to your children that you do not sincerely want to be true! Talk about what you want instead of what you don't want. Use your words to point people in the direction you want them to go. Here's what she could scream instead, "Walk, please! (My precious little darlings.)"

Unintentionally we can even reinforce what is negative or ineffective in another person. As with many of my best lessons, I learned this one from my son.

When Tabor was growing up, he tested the boundaries (bless his heart). In fact, he was a professional boundaries tester. If the curfew was midnight, he would push that just a bit to see what might happen. The short answer is, "I happen." (I was the mama at the door as he walked through it, greeting his late rear end.) Every Friday or Saturday night we would repeat this performance: He would be twenty minutes late, and I would deliver a twenty-minute lecture. "You do this every time. You are always pushing your toe over that line. You are always late!"

Then it dawned on me. I was reinforcing exactly what I did not want. I was locking my child into a negative pattern of behavior. With that realization, I was determined not to continue the dysfunctional pattern. I devised a new plan, and part of me hoped he would be a little late very soon so I could try it out.

He did not disappoint. The very next Saturday, he came schlepping through the door a full twenty-five minutes after the appointed time. I said, "Tabor, this is not like you. I was very worried." I wish I could insert a picture here of the look on his face. He was absolutely astonished.

He said, "What are you talking about? This is what I do. This is what we do."

Then my plan kicked into full gear. Calmly I said, "No, this is not what we *do*, and this is not who you *are*. You are a respectful person—a man of your word. You care about your family, and you would never do anything purposely to worry or disrespect me." With that I went to bed. (Deeply satisfied with myself, I might add.)

I don't know how long he stood there trying to figure out what had just happened to him. Perhaps someday I'll ask.

This scene was repeated over the next several weeks. He would be late, and I would remind him, "This is not like you. This is not who you are. You are a man of your word and a person of strong character." He was quite bewildered and not at all sure what to do with this new (improved) mother. Then his behavior began to change.

He began *syncing with the blessing*—reaching for the higher expectation. He started to be on time!

Today my son would tell you that being on time is not about schedules or rules. It is about respect and concern and character. Punctuality is a strong value for him as an adult. Being late for him is a *worst-case scenario*—something to be avoided at all cost.

Just as parents have the opportunity to bless their children, managers bless employees when they build positive expectations into the workplace and into the people they lead. It is possible (and profitable) to breathe success into the work culture. There are a number of ways leaders communicate performance expectations. Certainly job requirements and performance targets set expectations, and that is only the beginning.

Another way leaders set expectations is in what they believe people are capable of. We know that extraordinary leaders expect extraordinary things from the people they lead—they breathe those expectations into every communication. It has the "Pygmalion Effect."

In George Bernard Shaw's play *Pygmalion*, Professor Henry Higgins claims that he can take a common flower girl—someone of low social standing—and, with rigorous training, pass her off as a duchess. He succeeds, but inside the story is a key performance principle—Eliza Doolittle makes this comment to the professor's friend Pickering:

You see, really and truly, apart from the things anyone can pick up (the dressing and the proper way of speaking, and so on), the difference between a lady and a flower girl is not how she behaves, but how she's treated. I shall always be a flower girl to Professor Higgins, because he always treats me as a flower girl, and always will; but I know I can be a lady to you, because you always treat me as a lady, and always will.[1]

In dozens of ways every day we reflect and communicate our expectations. Without even realizing it, we send cues and clues to others about what we expect from them, what we think they are capable of, and what we believe about their potential. Expectations are also reflected in what we pay attention to and what we ignore. It is in the feedback we give (or don't give). All of this has a distinct and powerful impact on performance, results, and job satisfaction.[2]

Leaders communicate expectations by the work they assign, how much and what they trust employees with, whom they include, and how they include them. A leader may ask the team for ideas to solve a problem, or a leader might simply give the team a list of tasks that have already been decided. Both of those approaches signal expectations. The first approach says, "I trust your ability to solve this issue. I want your ideas." The second says, "Just do what I say, because I know best. I believe in me more than I believe in you."

As you can see, in our personal and professional lives we are constantly revealing our expectations. In this way, we quite literally set the bar—for ourselves, for others, and even for the organizations for which we work. Ask yourself the following questions to discover how you are communicating and creating expectations at home and at work:

- What do you believe about and expect from others?

- What do you think others are capable (or not capable) of?

- How are you communicating those expectations directly and indirectly?

- How might you be reinforcing what is negative and limiting?

- How are you locking others into unproductive attitudes and behaviors?

- What seeds of belief are you sowing with your words? Just as beliefs have been planted into your life by what others have spoken, your words will fall onto the soil of the hearts around you.

My experience with locking people into low performance with my expectations was nothing short of remarkable. Years ago, I was complaining (blatantly whining, actually) to my boss about a nonperforming employee. It was a persistent problem, and I was quite frustrated. He listened for a moment, and then said, "Describe the communication you have with your top-performing employee."

That was easy! The top performer on the team was an absolute pleasure. My communications with her were frequent, open, and relaxed. I looked forward to speaking with her. When I saw her car in the parking lot, I would think, "Good, she's here!"

Then my boss asked me to describe the pattern of communication with the low performer. Dramatically I threw myself back in the chair and rolled my eyes. "I dread it," I sighed. "She exasperates me. Thinking about her exhausts me. I am getting tired right now. When I see her car in the parking lot, I want to bang my head on the steering wheel." Communication with the low performer was tense, guarded, and only when absolutely necessary!

The wisdom in what he said next floored me. Without a trace of judgment he asked, "Is your communication with the top performer because she is performing, or is she performing because of her relationship with you? Which came first, the relationship or the performance? What if you were able to duplicate that kind of communication with the nonperformer? What do you suppose would happen to her performance?"

It's an interesting question, don't you think?

With nothing to lose, I decided to find out. For several weeks, I concentrated on communicating with the low performer as if she were a top performer. I interacted with her more often. I went out of my way to greet her. I asked for her opinion on an issue I was struggling with. I stated my confidence in her ability to succeed. I looked for opportunities to recognize her, and I vividly described the difference I believed she could make for the team.

Slowly at first, then with building momentum, her attitude and performance began to shift. This underperforming employee went on to become a top producer on the team. She stepped into the vision of performance I had spoken over her.

What a profound lesson in leadership. I wish I could say that every performance issue can be solved by changing the pattern of communication. That isn't realistic, but it is certainly a great place to start. This employee responded almost immediately to the message of victory and success, and she was not the only person to change.

I changed too. That's the beauty of the blessing. It always impacts the one who sends it and the one who receives it.

Ultimately all blessings flow from God. As Diana Hagee teaches in her book of proclamations, "We must declare God's position over every situation in our lives. The phrase 'to proclaim' comes from the Latin, which means to 'shout forth.'"[3] We are to shout forth a declaration of victory in every situation and area of our lives.

Many of my proclamations are scriptures—the timeless, unchanging promises of God. I write them on index cards and carry them with me. On one of my proclamation cards is written:

I am blessed and highly favored in every area of my life—in my home, my family, my work, and my health. The favor of God goes before me and rests upon me. I fully expect the favor of God in everything I do and everywhere I go.

Proclamations like this lift your head, fill your heart with hope, and remind you what God has already said about your life and your future. They do something else too. These declarations usher in a bigger dream...a greater vision for your life.

## JOURNALING EXERCISE

I encourage you to declare absolute victory in every area of your life with bold proclamations!

1. What does absolute victory look like in your finances, relationships, career, spiritual life, marriage, children, education, and physical health?

2. Review your list of worries. What would victory look like in each of these situations? (By now you have probably imagined the absolute worst in these scenarios. I invite you to vividly imagine and describe victory.)

3. Create a proclamation for each one. Your proclamation or blessing is a statement of absolute faith. It speaks in the present tense as if the blessing has already arrived. It says, "I am...," not, "I will be someday."

4. Read your proclamations aloud every day (even when you don't feel like it).

# 11

# GRAND DESIGNS

*Daring to dream*

H ERE'S A BOLD QUESTION: If you could do anything, and you knew you could not fail, what would you try? When I ask that question, more often than not I get a blank stare! We aren't used to thinking like this. Or maybe we've forgotten how.

Do you remember your dreams?

I've heard people say, "I had a dream," or "I have forgotten how to dream." Some tell me they were never encouraged to dream, and they don't know how. These people have more or less settled for what came by. They've handled well what has been passed to them, but they did not understand they could reach for something more or different.

Others admit they have put their dreams on hold, waiting for the perfect conditions—for the children to be raised, for finances to be better, and for the moon to be perfectly aligned with Mars. Waiting for perfect conditions really means the time for a bigger dream will never come.

Many of us are just too busy to dream. We have a dozen *must-dos*, and dreaming never quite reaches the top of the pile. I ache when people say, "I'm afraid to dream," or "I lost my dream, and it's too late for me."

Marjorie, a woman in her sixties, believes it is too late for her to have a dream or accomplish anything extraordinary. "Time has passed me by," she told me quietly. "I have spent my life taking care of everyone else, and I was happy to do that. But my arms are empty now. I don't have a purpose, and it is too late in the game to find one."

This precious woman believes that her life has been spent and there are no opportunities left. She believes she has missed her chance at doing or creating something of real value. Perhaps more tragic than that, she believes she has invested herself in the common and mundane.

What do you think would happen to Marjorie if she believed something more powerful about her past and her future? What do you think would happen if you did the same?

Perhaps when we were small, it was more natural to dream of big things. We thought we could be anything (including superheroes). Then we grew up. Our bodies got bigger, and our dreams got smaller. We learned how to settle, and we learned how to fail. We became more realistic, super responsible, and a little (or more than a little) cynical.

We started believing it when people said, "That's impossible." We got busy, tired, and overwhelmed. The business of life choked the life out of our dreams.

If you can relate to that, I hope this book inspires you to dream a big dream again. Maybe we have to go back in time to accomplish that, back to when being a superhero actually sounded reasonable—back to a time when we thought we could change the world and the most amazing things were possible.

*Maybe a really big dream begins with four words we loved to hear as children: "Once upon a time..."*

Perhaps we need a new life story.

Stories have always been used to teach, motivate, and inspire. In the Bible, parables were used to make powerful points, move the heart, and ignite the spirit. We use stories to instruct children because they capture attention and spark the imagination. Much of the work I do is teaching corporate leaders how to use stories and metaphors to communicate the vision and share a vivid picture of success with the workforce.

Great stories are memorable. They resonate with an audience—even an audience of one. A really great story will change you forever. In this information-overloaded world, stories are a powerful way to carry the message.

Daring to dream is like writing a story. What is the story you would write about your future? What does that vision look like? I encourage you to write your story, because there is a huge difference between a life with vision and a life without it. The story you tell about your future is like a road map. An old map will take us to an old place. If we want to move beyond the old boundaries, we must create a new map, with a new story.

In his book *The Power of Story*, Jim Loehr has this to say about our life stories:

> They may or may not inspire us to take hope-filled action to better our lives. They may or may not take us where we ultimately want to go. But since our destiny follows our stories, it's imperative that we do everything in our power to get our stories right. For most of us that means some serious editing.[1]

This is true at a personal level, and it is true in at organizational level. Organizations who have not carefully crafted and communicated the story wonder why employees are not engaged, committed, and motivated. It is because the employees do not have a vision of the future. They do not feel connected to something larger than themselves. They do not share a common, compelling purpose. They do not see themselves as potential heroes in an exciting plot, and they certainly do not feel powerful enough to alter the outcome of the story.

Where there is no vision, people will indeed perish (Prov. 29:18). In our personal lives, perishing looks like eking it out, expecting less, and accepting what comes. At work, perishing is showing up, doing just enough to collect a paycheck, and going home exhausted and disillusioned.

That is not so in organizations with a powerful vision of the future. Here people are connected to a higher purpose. They understand how their work impacts the big picture. They are investing in something beyond themselves. Purpose gives the work context.

I love the story of a consultant who visited NASA. As he walked through the entrance into the lobby, he saw a woman scrubbing the floor. The consultant asked her, "What is your job at NASA?"

I thought this was a ridiculous question. It's perfectly obvious what this woman does for NASA. But her answer changed my mind. She proudly replied, "I help put people on the moon."

This woman actually believes that she had something to do with putting people on the moon! You know what? She does. She has the nerve to think they could not do it without her. And she's absolutely right.

Because she is connected to the big picture, this woman works with a different spirit. I believe she stands taller when they launch at NASA. That has nothing to do with a paycheck. It has everything to do with being connected to (and ignited by) a very big dream.

Organizations need a powerful vision of the future to ignite passion and purpose in people. The same is true for individuals. We need a clear and compelling picture of the future to transcend what is mundane and mediocre. We were not designed to simply exist! We were made with purpose for a great purpose.

Here's the real difference a big dream makes: It is entirely possible to know *what* to do and even *how* to do it really well. But if you forget *why*, the meaning drains away. That's a huge problem for organizations today. They have employees who know what to do and know how to do it, but they have forgotten why it matters. They are not engaged at an emotional level. They bring their heads and hands to work, but they leave their hearts at the door!

*A big dream (for organizations and for individuals) is the why behind the how and the what.*

If you do not have a sense of your purpose now, it simply means you haven't found it. Maybe it means you haven't searched it out. Perhaps you haven't been asking the question, "What is my dream? What is my God-given legacy? What is the story I want to write with my life?"

I promise that if you begin asking the question, your answer will come. Keep on asking until it does. A dear woman in my life recently said to me, "I don't have a dream, and I don't know how to get one." I told to her ask for one. Pray for a bigger dream, and keep praying until you get one.

God has a big dream and a big plan for your life. He has already declared it. He has planted the seeds of that dream into your heart. Look to your skills, your strengths, and your heart's desires. Think about your talents, your interests, and your personality style. These are important clues for your life story. Those gifts and preferences were not planted inside of you by accident. They were placed there purposefully to equip you in accomplishing your mission.

Remember—it is not too late for you to write an extraordinary life story! The most wonderful stories have fabulous middles and incredible endings, even if the beginning wasn't exactly what you had in mind. You have the power to write a new story with your life, and it is never too soon or too late to begin.

I encourage you to dream a bigger dream and to encourage the ones you love to do the same. That vision will infuse you with purpose, ignite your passion, renew your commitment, and motivate you to action. The action part is important. As you will see in the chapter to come, this book isn't about hoping for a bigger dream; it is about *achieving one.*

## JOURNALING EXERCISE

1. Review your list of beliefs, including those you have exchanged or added along the way. If these

beliefs were assigned to the characters in a story, what would the characters be like?

2. What would be the theme and the plot of this story?

3. Take a run at dreaming bigger. What would you try if success were absolutely guaranteed?

4. What gifts and strengths have been planted inside of you? What role do they play in your vision?

5. What is the story you would like to write with your life?

# 12

# MAKING IT REAL

*Setting and achieving goals*

I MEET SO MANY PEOPLE who long to do more with their lives. They have pieces of a vision, but they don't know how or where to begin. Too often the dream has been placed on a shelf—like memorabilia of the heart. It's pretty to look at, but we're not quite sure what to do with it! If that describes you, I encourage you to pull your dream out, blow the dust off of it, and practice the goal-setting steps in this chapter.

> Write the vision and make it plain on tablets.
> —HABAKKUK 2:2, NKJV

The most successful people have their goals written down, and they review them every single day. The moment you put your goals in writing, you engage the reticular activating system in your brain. That means your brain is now on high alert, looking for and searching out the people, opportunities, and information to achieve the goal.

You'll notice an article on the cover of a magazine with the information you've been looking for. You'll be introduced to people who can help you. You'll stumble across amazing opportunities. The truth is that those miraculous things may have happened anyway, but you just wouldn't have noticed or connected with them because your goals weren't written down and in the front of your mind. I am convinced that opportunities walked right by us yesterday, and have perhaps walked right by us even today. We didn't see them because we weren't looking for them.

That gives a new meaning to the adage: "When the student is ready, the teacher will appear." When you write your goals down, you're getting ready—you are planting seeds of opportunity and success.

## LEVELS OF GOALS

We have already talked about having a grand design or vision for your life. These are God-born dreams for a life and a legacy. To get there you will also need short-term, mid-term, and long-term goals.

- Set short-term goals for up to one year.

- Reach out three to five years with mid-term goals.

- Extend your reach even further with long-term goals spanning ten years or more.

At each of these levels, you steadily move closer to the ultimate vision—the story you are writing with your life. The goals you have for this year and the goals for three to ten years from now are the small steps you take toward the grand design. What may feel like a *shoebox-sized* plan will grow into a breathtakingly beautiful garden, one that you will look upon with great expectancy with each passing season of your life.

Make your goals very specific. Bring them into focus, and create a clear picture of the end result. Instead of saying, "I want a *new house*," describe the house in great detail. It is a two-story, French country design, with four bedrooms, and sits on a lake! Rather than saying, "I want a *better job*," describe the job. What is the title, compensation, and job description? If going back to school is your goal, what degree are you going to earn, and when will you graduate?

Seeing the end result in detail is essential. If you cannot see that picture in your mind's eye, you cannot get there. You must be able to picture the finish line and imagine yourself crossing it. If you have a big goal, and it is difficult for you to imagine yourself in that future place, you may need to break it up into smaller pieces—pieces you can imagine. These smaller successes will enable you to imagine greater and greater accomplishments over time.

We can learn a lot from the experience of Florence Chadwick. In 1954 on the Fourth of July, she set out to swim from Catalina Island to the California coast. She was already the first woman to swim the English Channel in both directions, and this would be another first for women in history.

As the story goes, she had been in the icy water for hours. The dense fog swallowed her sight. She couldn't see the boats following alongside, and she couldn't see the distant shore. Her mother and her trainer shouted encouragement from a boat next to her. They assured her the shore was near, but she could not see it.

Less than half a mile from the shore, Florence did something she had never done. She quit. Exhausted, she was pulled from the freezing water.

What happened to Florence Chadwick has probably happened to each of us in some way. She could not see the shoreline in the fog. She lost sight of her goal and gave up just short of reaching it. Exhaustion and discouragement overcame her, even though others were cheering her on.

That is not the end of the story. Two months later, Florence Chadwick dove into the Catalina Channel again with a goal to make history. In spite of the dense fog, she was successful. In her mind, she held a picture of the shore she could not see with her eyes.[1]

Florence Chadwick reminds us to memorize our own *distant shores*, so that no matter what happens, our vision is not obstructed. We can move steadily forward with complete confidence and faith. The fog may roll in, and we may grow weary. Even so, we are sure our destination—our victory—is there, closer than we may know. We will not lose sight of the goal, because the goal is on the inside of us.

I recommend that you use index cards to record your goals. On one side of the card, describe your victory in vivid detail. On the other side, list the resources you'll need to be successful, people who can help, and the actions you can take to move in the direction of your goal. Carry these cards with you, and read them aloud every single day.

This is a success secret. Many people have worthy, even exciting aspirations. Only a small percentage of them actually put these in writing and consistently read them. The moment you take these steps, you have separated yourself from the multitude that stops with a dream. You give your dream strong legs to run on.

## TESTING YOUR GOALS

You will also want to test your goals. Make sure they are real and are really yours. Test your goals with questions like these:

- Why do I want to have this, do this, or become this?

- How will achieving this goal contribute to my *grand design?*

- How will accomplishing this goal make a difference?

- What will my life look like if I don't achieve this goal?

Some of your goals won't pass this test. Ultimately you may realize they are expectations others have of you, or they are just neat ideas that will not survive the heat of adversity. If the goal isn't real, when you encounter obstacles or resistance, you'll fold. You will give up.

Testing your goals is important, because achieving them will cost you something. Your goals will stretch you and take you out of your comfort zone. They will challenge you and stimulate growth. Worthy goals are an investment of your resources—time, money, energy, and creativity.

Recently, my husband and I attended a health and wellness seminar in San Antonio. The doctor introduced his lecture by asking each person to write his or her personal *why* on an index card. Why do you want to be healthier? The *why*, he explained, is your motivation.

If you cannot articulate your personal why, you will not succeed in making the changes necessary to accomplish the goal. You will not be relentlessly committed to success.

Once you've written your goals down and tested them, once you have clarified your *why*, it's time to build a plan of action. This is clearly outlining the steps you will take to achieve your goal.

After leaving a meeting at work about changes in compensation, Beth had this to say: "I knew it wasn't going to be good news, and I was right. This change in compensation really amounts to a $400-a-month cut in pay. I am barely making ends meet now, and I don't know what I am going to do."

Beth's first response was to focus on what she would be losing. That is certainly understandable, but it is not a goal. It is fear. I asked her, "What amount do you need to live comfortably? What are your financial goals?"

She wasn't used to thinking about her finances that way. "I've been doing the math backward," she realized. "I have been focusing on what I get and what I must do to make that go around."

Once she established financial goals for the short, mid, and long term, Beth created an action plan. Her plan included becoming debt free, building her savings, and increasing her discretionary income. She negotiated with her employer for more flexible work hours and the opportunity to work from home two days a week. These arrangements allowed her to reduce commuting and day-care expenses and spend more time with her children. These steps and others are taking her steadily to her financial goals. She feels in control of her finances for the first time in her life.

As she reflects on the change in compensation, Beth realizes it was actually a positive catalyst. "My goals and action plan uncovered options I hadn't even considered. The goals gave me a sense of personal control and greater financial discipline. Instead of passively accepting what my employer wanted to give or take away, I focused on the actions I can take and what I personally control. I am more financially disciplined now, but not because I can't spend money. I'm just making different financial choices—choices that line up with my goals."

Beth's story is a good example of how goals change our focus and empower us. Goals have the ability to move us from fear to action, and, in Beth's case, from barely making it to achieving peace of mind and financial freedom.

Reaching for your goal will require resource management. As you define your personal victories, consider what you will need to be successful. Resources may include time, money, information, skills, and even people. Below are seven questions you can ask to identify your resources:

1. What do you need to learn more about?

2. What skills will you need to acquire?

3. Who has accomplished a goal like this?

4. What steps did they take to make it happen?

5. What financial resources will you need?

6. Whose support will you require?

7. How much time will you set aside to accomplish this goal?

As your plan comes together, you may feel overwhelmed by the scope of it. You may feel that you don't have all of the resources you need to fully engage in your dream. If that is true, I would ask you this: How can you begin to experience a piece of your dream now?

One of my goals is to own a horse. This has been a dream of mine since I was a child. With my travel schedule and other commitments, owning a horse is not entirely practical. So, I continued to dream of someday having one. That is until my husband purchased riding privileges at a ranch in San Antonio. I can ride anytime (and I don't have to scoop poop, trim feet, or worry about proper horse diets and shoes). I just get to enjoy a little piece of my dream now. It's one more thing that I am doing instead of dreaming, and I like that.

When people tell me they want a degree but cannot go back to school full-time, I encourage them to take a night class or an online course, meet with an advisor to map out a plan, or attend a seminar that may count toward the credits required.

Perhaps you dream of starting a business, but you need your day job! Begin by learning everything you can about the business you are interested in. Become a student of the industry, build a network of contacts, and interview people who are doing what you dream of. Write your business plan, develop your goals, and elect your board of directors!

In each of these examples, the point is to begin. Perhaps you cannot dive into the deep end of your dream just now. Then put a toe in the water. Be creative as you search for ways to experience what you've been dreaming about.

Don't be surprised if your goals require some adjusting along the way. As you advance and grow, you will see farther down the road. Your perspective will change, and your vision will increase. Course corrections are a normal part of the process, so evaluate your progress frequently and update your plans to stay on target.

## SET YOUR STONES

Progress produces hope. When we see ourselves moving closer to the goal, we get our second and third wind! Make your progress visible. Set your stones.

In biblical times, people were often instructed to build memorials as reminders of significant events. Memorials were built to mark a journey completed, a victory won, faith tested, lessons learned, and power revealed. They were set with stones, written in books, captured in song, and kept with feasts.

The people were instructed to remember these significant events in many ways—do not forget what you have been through, what you have learned, and what you have seen. Do not forget the miracles that brought you here, and tell these stories to your children.

> Let this be a sign among you, so that when your children ask later, saying, "What do these stones mean to you?" then you shall say to them, "Because the waters of the Jordan were cut off before the ark of the covenant of the LORD; when it crossed the Jordan, the waters of the Jordan were cut off." So these stones shall become a memorial to the sons of Israel forever.
>
> —JOSHUA 4:6–7, NAS

You are on a journey as well. You will reach goals and win victories. Your faith will be tested, you will learn the most marvelous things, and you will witness power—miracles even. Take the time to fully experience all of these things and build your memorials.

In our home is a wall of crosses. On the back of each one is a date and an event. Some of the crosses mark a victory; others honor a heartbreak that we have successfully come through. Each one is precious, and after years of marking our journey in this way, the wall tells an amazing story. It is a story of triumph and tears, of miracles and great hope. These are the prayers we have prayed and the answers we've seen.

I heard of a family who is building a garden wall. Every year on Thanksgiving Day they gather stones to mark significant events. Each member of the family is encouraged to etch a stone and place it into the wall. What a wonderful tradition!

Your journal is a memorial. It is a map of your journey—the questions you've asked and the answers you've found. Look back through the pages and see where you've been! It's an amazing process unfolding before you. The changes may be so subtle you barely notice, but when you look back over time, you see how far you have come and how much you have grown.

I encourage you to mark your journey and set your memorial stones. Find a way to measure your progress and celebrate your growth. Do this for you and for those who will come after. Then when they ask, "What are these stones?" you will tell a story of hope.

Remember that smaller consistent changes are generally more effective than radical shifts. That's one of the reasons New Year's resolutions and crash diets fail so miserably. Planning to hit the gym every day probably isn't realistic if we haven't been there in a year! It is better to turn small changes into habits that will really stick. A better goal might be to increase whatever I am doing now by 15–20 percent for a few weeks. Once that becomes my normal routine, I can raise the bar incrementally until I am where I want to be.

Ultimately I have learned that God is the source of the dream and the success. I like it when God trusts me with big stuff. If He brings me to it, I know He will provide the resources to accomplish it. I also believe that God is just as interested in the process as He is in the achievement. In other words, what we become in pursuit of the goal may be the whole point after all. Meaningful goals will change you in meaningful ways. Your destination is the goal, but there is always real purpose in the trip!

## JOURNALING EXERCISE

1. What are the *whys* behind your goals?

2. How can you begin to experience a piece of your dream today?

3. How can you help someone else experience a piece of his or her dream?

4. How will you set your stones?

# 13

# FIND YOUR BALANCE AND PROTECT YOUR PLAN

*Align your life*

JUGGLING IS HARD. SOMETIMES to illustrate time management principles, I'll give a brief juggling lesson. Everyone in the audience is invited to try their hand at keeping three tennis balls in constant motion. I ask them to imagine the balls are values, goals, and commitments. Their mission is to keep all of these moving smoothly through the air. With practice, they should be able to do it effortlessly!

What follows is complete mayhem and absolute chaos. Most people end up breathlessly searching for commitments under banquet tables and chairs. Some of these have never been recovered! (If you attend a conference and find a tennis ball rolling around under the table, it may very well be one of these wayward goals!)

It's a realistic metaphor, don't you think? Managing life's commitments can feel a lot like a juggling act. One priority is always falling in order to lift another. In those terms, juggling does not work as a great analogy for designing one's life.

When first learning to juggle, people often use scarves. They are easier to manage, and they don't get away from you quite so easily. The problem with *real-life* juggling is that what we are trying to manage *does get away from us*! We aren't juggling scarves. We are juggling our commitments, relationships, finances, emotions, and health (just to name a few). Some of the balls we are trying to keep in the air will bounce if we drop them. Some of them don't bounce;

they shatter. And it may surprise you, but some of them we actually need to drop!

I am sure you've heard the caution, "Don't drop the ball." We learn early in life that *dropping the ball* is a bad thing. (The underlying message is, "Don't fail. Don't let us down.") As it relates to finding your balance, dropping the ball (on purpose) may actually be the right thing—the most effective thing to do after all. It means you are making conscious choices about what you will and will not commit to. It means that you are willing to do what it takes to protect what you value the most.

It's not always easy to drop the ball—even when you are doing it on purpose. We want to please. We want to feel in control. We feel guilty when we say no. That's why we end up saying yes to the wrong things and find ourselves spinning out of control. In trying to keep the wrong things *up in the air,* we may even drop the right things, the most valuable things.

Trisha is a young mother with a demanding career and a deep desire to do it all well. "I have a very competitive nature. I want to be the best at everything—the best mom, the best employee, the best wife, and the best volunteer. Nothing but the best is good enough for me," she laughs.

Trisha was the president of the local PTA, actively involved in several professional associations, and a well-known volunteer in the community. All of this worked for a little while. Then she noticed something important—she wasn't enjoying any of it. Trisha found that activity and achievement do not equal satisfaction and fulfill-ment. "I learned that sometimes *a little* really is *more.* When you try to be everything to everyone, you end up shortchanging the whole lot. You let yourself and others down."

It was one thing to understand that; it was something entirely different to do something about it. "It was excruciating to snip the strings of these commitments," Trisha recalls. "And it was humbling too. That's when I realized how much of my identity was tangled up in the activity. If I stopped doing all of these things, who would I be? How important would I be?"

Trisha's real problem wasn't an overstuffed schedule. It was definition and design. She was defining herself and her worth through corporate and community titles; she wasn't designing a life around what she valued most.

"Learning how to say no was the easy part," she remembers. "The hard part was understanding that my personal worth is not calculated by the number of committees I sit on or the title on my business card. I spent a great deal of time with my collection of personal beliefs. Some of them had to go!"

As Trisha learned, the first step in designing a life is to consciously decide what you really value. When asked, people often have a spontaneous list of values: faith, family, health, wealth, security, making a real difference, creativity—even power and fame.

Once you have defined or clarified your values, look at your time and action. Are your values reflected in what you do? Once you decide what is most important, balance is really just protecting and promoting what you value. If not, what needs adjusting?

1. If family is at the top of your list, how many appointments on your calendar have a family member's name next to them? When something has to give in your schedule, how often is it the people you live with, the people you value the most?

2. If you have named health as a top priority, how much of your attention and time is dedicated to wellness? What health goals have you set for yourself, and how are you progressing toward those? What disciplines are you building? How are you investing yourself in your health?

3. If you place extreme value on faith, what are you doing to build and grow spiritually?

Ultimately we all answer the question, "What do I value most?" We answer by the choices we make. Our time, actions, and energy should reflect what we value. If they don't, something must change—either we must change our focus or become more honest about what we really value. This is critical, because living outside of what you value creates internal conflict, stress, a sense of failure, and, as medical research contends, even chronic medical problems.[1]

A woman with chronic stomach pain visited her doctor regularly. With each appointment, she arrived breathless, exhausted, and more than a little frustrated with her family. Time and again she told the doctor how hard it was to keep her home clean and looking presentable with three small children.

After several visits (always with the same stomach pain and the same complaints), the doctor asked her, "What do you value most in life? What is most important to you?"

She answered immediately, without hesitation, "My family, of course."

Her doctor disagreed, and he told her so. "Your family is not the most important thing. A perfect home in perfect order is your true priority." Before she could argue the point, he went on to say, "You are living outside of your values. What you say is most important is not what you do. If your family really is the most important thing, then you must stop worrying about a perfect home. If a perfect home is truly what you care about, you must finally admit that to yourself."

This woman left the doctor's office with a lot on her mind. Almost immediately the transformation began. She stopped obsessing about the house as much and started enjoying her children more. Her actions aligned with her values, and the stomach pain took care of itself.

Once again we see that mind, body, and spirit connection. Sometimes physical symptoms even point to a lack of alignment between our values and our time. Again it's a little like cars in an intersection. If we are not well aligned, there will be a collision between what we say we value and what we put first. When things collide, there is damage.

Ultimately, the most successful lives have carefully selected priorities and values that are balanced. Here are five strategies to find your balance and, yes, to drop some of those balls!

1. *Set goals.* Balance first comes through realistic goal setting. When you have a clear vision for your life and have outlined that vision with goals, it is easier to set priorities and make good decisions about time and commitments. Time management experts would say, "You cannot make good choices about where to spend your time if you don't know what the priorities are." To align your life with your values, set goals for the important *compartments* of your life (family, community, financial, spiritual, health, and career, for example).

2. *Let go.* Balance also comes when you let go of the need to control. In trying to control everything, you will actually spin out of control. In what situations do you need to let go and trust others more?

3. *Get help!* That really means you must get over the notion that you have to constantly *prove* yourself at work and at home. Get as much help as you can hire, bargain, or negotiate for!

4. *Delegate more.* I call this the *Subtraction List*. Most of us are pretty good at adding, but we aren't as skilled at subtracting. What are you doing that doesn't add real value? What are you doing that someone else could be

(or should be) doing? How are you actually treating your family and co-workers to overrely on you and underrely on themselves? At work, ask yourself this sobering question: "Would I pay someone what I make to do what I am doing right now?" It is an interesting question, to be sure.

5. *Get closure!* Close the loop, and take care of unfinished business. Say what needs saying, do what needs doing, and forgive what needs forgiving. We cannot move on to the next step until we master the one we are on. This is true in every area of our lives.

## THE BALANCE WHEEL

The balance wheel is a tangible way to evaluate how well aligned and balanced you are in your life compartments. Below is an illustration of the wheel, labeled with what many people consider the most

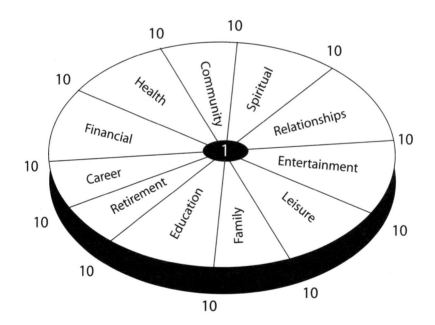

important pieces of life. As you put the pieces together, the life is whole. As you draw the pie or the wheel for your life, you may choose to label the pieces differently, and you might have a different number of pieces that make the whole of your life.

Now take a look at the second wheel. Imagine this is the wheel of your life. Label each *piece* in the wheel that depicts your life. The spokes will be used to measure the current condition in each area of your life. At the center of the wheel is a "1." At the end of each spoke is a "10." On a scale from one to ten, with ten being the best, place a notch on each spoke to indicate where you see yourself in that area. Questions like these will help you determine your current score.

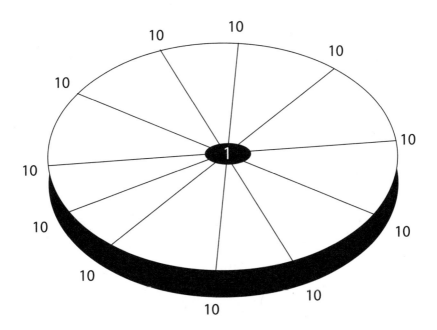

1. If you have goals for each compartment of your life, how are you progressing in each area?

2. What is the current condition of each *piece* of your life?

3. How satisfied are you with the effort you are making and the results you are getting?

After evaluating each area, connect the notches. This is a picture of the wheel your life is riding on! How bumpy or smooth will the ride be? How small is your wheel? When we travel on very small wheels, it takes more effort to go the distance! Is your wheel flat in some areas? What needs to change?

For most of us, an exercise like this will point to areas of our life that need more focus or attention. We may need to renew commitments, adjust our priorities, or formulate goals to achieve the balance we would like to see.

## ALLOW YOURSELF A SEASON OF REST

And don't store away the crops that grow on their own or gather the grapes from your unpruned vines. The land must have a year of complete rest.

—LEVITICUS 25:5

There will be times in your life when nothing seems to be happening. The project is complete, the goal has been achieved, and skills have been tested. You have navigated a significant or difficult change. You've pushed through the obstacles...and then nothing. You may even feel like you've been put on the shelf—set aside and forgotten. You may wonder if all of your hard work was in vain.

Maybe you've had the gas pedal to the floor for so long you don't even know how to slow down. Your wheel looks more like the one whirling around in a hamster's cage! With all of our mobile, work-from-home, at-the-beach, or on-the-plane gadgets, it's hard to disconnect.

I see hardworking people go from project to project without missing a beat. When I speak to groups of employees, they so relate to this! They move heaven and earth to meet a deadline—working ridiculous hours and sacrificing balance in their lives. Once complete, that deadline is replaced with another, then another after that. There is no finish line! "We are never done," they say.

There will be times when you acquire balance through rest. *Allow yourself these seasons; they have tremendous purpose in your life.* Seeds know about seasons; inside of each one the potential waits to burst forth at just the right moment.

Farmers understand that if you work the soil for too long without alternating the pattern, you will drain the land of its ability to produce. At times the land is left to lie with nothing planted and nothing harvested for a time. Or farmers will alternate what is planted. Rotating the crops changes which nutrients are drawn from the soil and what is left behind at the harvest. Resting the soil is a purposeful, strategic investment in the future.

We would be wise to understand this process in our own lives. I asked a colleague once, "Do you feel guilty when you are not working?"

She responded instantly, "Only when I'm not working."

We must learn to rest our soil—alternate the pattern—so what is drawn from us does not drain us of our ability to produce. As you work to acquire balance in your own life, or if you are leading others, I encourage you to find and celebrate the finish lines. Take your foot off the gas pedal and step off of the wheel for a moment. Have the wisdom to know when the best strategy, the winning strategy, is to rest.

## JOURNALING EXERCISE

1. What kind of wheel are you riding on now?
2. How well are your commitments aligned with your goals?
3. Where are you out of alignment? What areas need more attention to balance your wheel?
4. Which balls need to drop?
5. What can you do to rest the soil of your life?

# BROKEN FENCES AND OPEN GATES

*Building productive boundaries*

D o you have a *border problem* in your life? Many people do. When you fail to establish boundaries or maintain your *gates and fences*, you invite people to *trespass*, and that places a strain on relationships and results.

Borders aren't for locking people out. Quite the opposite is true. Effective boundaries allow us to live, love, and work productively. They guard our self-respect, protect what we value, and allow us to ask for what we need. Without proper boundaries, personal and professional relationships are jeopardized. Eventually we will be hurt or feel taken advantage of and become resentful.

Life, love, and work without boundaries invite conflict, tension, and disappointment. Without boundaries you paint yourself into uncomfortable corners. Think of your boundaries as the best conflict prevention at your disposal! The old saying is true after all: "Good fences make good neighbors."

Boundaries can be difficult, because to protect them you may feel selfish, or feel that you are at risk for hurting someone's feelings. You may find yourself in conflict (which many of us go to great lengths to avoid). You may find it easier to establish boundaries with people you don't know well. It can be much more difficult to define the limits with people we are closest to or intimate with.

People who have a hard time establishing boundaries with others can relate to these warning signs:

- Losing objectivity

- Developing a warped sense of responsibility

- Being easily manipulated or controlled

- Feeling guilty, afraid, or lonely

- Fearing rejection or failure[1]

Dr. Nancy Allison describes boundary problems this way:

> Persons with unclear boundaries establish the "locus of control" outside themselves. They allow others to define who they are, what they think, where they go. Intimacy for this individual can easily lead to abuse if those with whom they relate prove untrustworthy.[2]

We certainly do not want others to define us, think for us, or manipulate us! We would not purpose to lose our objectivity or develop a warped sense of responsibility. If we are passive about our boundaries, we risk doing all of the above.

Boundaries are the limits you establish with others to stand up for yourself, protect what you value, and teach others how to treat you. Essentially, boundaries are your gates and borders. They are your *yeses* and your *nos*—they are your fence lines and your gates.

The yeses in your life are the things you want and need. These are things you value and have decided you are worthy of and can ask for. Find your yeses by completing this sentence:

It is OK for me to:

- Have thirty minutes to *decompress* after work before starting dinner.

- Feel respected and appreciated.

- Receive credit and recognition for the work I do.

Stop for just a moment and list at least five of your yeses. If you find this hard to do, it doesn't mean you don't have wants and needs! It probably means you haven't taken the time to define them (or perhaps you haven't given yourself permission to ask for them). You have just discovered the first step in setting boundaries—it is building awareness around what you want, need, and value.

Find your nos in much the same way.

It is not OK for others to:

- Take advantage of me.

- Ridicule me.

- Take credit for my work.

What are your nos? As you make this list, you are experiencing the second step of boundary setting. Here you move from being aware of and defining your needs to deciding you deserve to have those needs met. It is OK to ask for these things. It is also OK to raise your hand when something is not working!

It's important to note that your boundaries do not control other people. Control isn't the purpose or the premise of boundary setting. In fact, when you set boundaries, you actually let go of the outcome. You tell the person, "This is how I feel, this is what I need, and this is what I am asking for." You are asking for a change in behavior. The other person involved retains the choice to change or remain the same. If the boundary is not honored, you decide whether or not to enforce it.

Abusive relationships are an extreme example of broken

boundaries. A woman may say to an abusive spouse, "I deserve to feel safe and respected in my home. I will not stay in an abusive relationship. If you hit me, I will call the police, I will press charges, and I will end this relationship."

If that boundary is not enforced, it is nothing more than an empty threat. That makes boundary setting in the future more difficult and less credible. While you don't control the actions of others, you do control your responses. You control defining the line and enforcing it. To be effective, you must be prepared to back up the boundaries you set. That produces personal credibility and confidence, and it teaches people how to treat you.

Sometimes our boundaries are undefined. We haven't established our *property lines*—our yeses and nos. When that is true, we aren't even aware the lines have been crossed until a major infraction has occurred. It is much more difficult (and painful) to establish boundaries after they have been compromised.

For some, the property lines move around. Today the fence is here. Tomorrow it will be there. Sometimes I will give you permission to climb right over the fence. (I might even give you a boost!)

Elaine works with a group of women who can be very negative. She does not want to be included in the whining, complaining, and gossip. This is a personal value and a boundary. Even so, she finds herself asking a co-worker who is pouting (again), "What's wrong?" The instant those words leave her lips she knows it was a big mistake.

*Whoosh!* The floodgate opens, and the co-worker jumps the fence—more than happy to share her toxic load. Elaine finds herself knee-deep in negative muck. As she walks away, her shoes are sticky. (She can almost hear them sloshing down the hall.) She schleps and sloshes all the way back to her desk, leaving pieces of her credibility behind. She had knocked a hole in her own fence and shouldn't be surprised if her co-workers wiggle through it next time.

Still other fences are invisible. These are like trip wire. I know where they are, but you don't. I shouldn't have to tell where the lines are drawn. (You should know where they are, because if your mother raised you right, it is perfectly obvious.)

Here's a story about invisible fences. A couple was celebrating a dozen years of wedded bliss. On the evening of their anniversary the husband told his wife, "I will take you anywhere you would like to go for dinner. You pick the place."

Sweetly she assures her husband, "Anywhere is fine, precious. You decide." (In her mind she is thinking, "Mona Lisa Fondue, and if you love me, you will know this.")

As they pull out of the driveway, he asks his beautiful bride, "Where would you like to go, love?" She pats his hand as she says, "Darling, as long as I am with you, anywhere is fine." The tune "Mona Lisa" is running through her mind as she thinks, "Get this right, pal."

He parks in front of her favorite restaurant, and she is overwhelmed with love for this wonderful, sensitive man. Her mood changes abruptly as her husband leads her into a restaurant she has never heard of across the street. She is furious! What an insensitive oaf. She doesn't tell her husband she is angry. (He should be able to figure that out on his own.)

When they leave the restaurant, she does not wait for her husband to open the car door. (She wants to do this herself, so she can slam it properly.) Trying to make sense of this sudden weather change, her husband reaches for her hand and asks, "What is it, dear? Did you not enjoy your dinner?"

This is too much for her! She lashes out, "I cannot believe we just had our anniversary dinner in THAT restaurant!"

Still trying to catch up, her bewildered husband asks, "Where did you want to go?"

She has just three words for him now, and she pushes them through tightly clenched teeth, "MONA LISA FONDUE!"

He has a fair question now. "Why didn't you tell me that?"

With that, she gathers up every ounce of indignation to deliver the crowning blow, "If I have to tell you, it doesn't count! You should just know. If you love me, you should just know."

What a ridiculous scene! But, honestly, can you relate to it? Have you ever *tested* your relationships with invisible fences?

Once we understand what boundaries are and how important they are, how do we establish them in our own lives? The following steps allow you to empower yourself with clear boundaries and find the lines that protect your values and your integrity.

1. List your yeses and nos. This may be difficult if you are thinking about them for the first time. Sometimes it's helpful to think of relationships that work well and relationships that don't. These real-life situations may help you define the lines. Remember to include the relationship you have with yourself! How well is that working? How do you honor and take care of you?

2. Reach below the yes or the no to understand why this is important to you. Look for core values below the boundary. What is the intention or goal of your boundary? What value does it protect or promote? Understanding the *why* of your boundary is important. It tests the validity of the boundary and strengthens your commitment to it.

3. When confronted with difficult situations, practice a boundaries communication with a friend or mentor.

Here are some sample boundary dilemmas. We can use them to illustrate the steps above.

- A friend in financial distress asks if she can move in with you. "After all, you don't have a roommate, and you do have a guest room." She is right—you don't have a roommate, because you don't want one! You value your space and privacy, and you've worked very hard to create that. You don't want your friend to move in, but that makes you feel selfish.

- A co-worker shares gossip about other team members. Even listening to this feels like a betrayal of trust, but you don't know what to say.

- A family member criticizes and belittles you every chance she gets. You bite your tongue and pretend not to take it seriously.

With scenarios like this it is easy to get sucked into the vortex of dysfunction! That's why I like communication models. (I like them a lot.) These are effective templates, especially when the stakes are high or when you are venturing out of your comfort zone. Communication steps provide pegs to hang your words on and bolster your confidence.

## THE TRIPLE A MODEL FOR THE BOUNDARIES TALK

The boundaries talk can certainly be uncomfortable. You are essentially saying no, and many people struggle with that. As one young professional said (after a difficult boundaries chat with a family member), "I feel selfish and mean."

I asked her how she would feel if the boundary were not established. She laughed and said, "Resentful and bitter!" I think we can agree the answer isn't to avoid the boundaries talk. We must find a way to say what needs saying effectively. (You will notice I didn't say *comfortably*. I said *effectively*. Comfort is not the goal!)

The triple A model is a really good tool for protecting your boundaries and feeling good about it. (Think of this model like a boundaries intervention.) You can tailor the model to your scenario by using the steps as an outline and inserting your script.

1. Acknowledge the situation or the request.

2. Assert yourself—speak to your values (without apology).

3. Ask a question that will keep the ownership where it belongs.

Here's how that might sound in our example of the friend asking to move in.

(Acknowledge) I know this has been a difficult time for you financially. (Assert) I value my privacy and space, and I am not looking for a roommate. (Ask) If you are looking for a roommate, there may be resources or services that can help you find the right situation. What options have you looked into?

This model may take some practice, and here are a few things you will want to keep in mind as you use it:

- When you assert your values, do not apologize for them! In our example, apology would have sounded something like, "I am so sorry, but I just can't have a roommate right now. I wish I could, but it just isn't a good time because..." This is what I call the *verbal wince*, and it undermines the entire message. When you insert the wince, you aren't believable. You don't sound like you believe in what you are saying or in your right to be saying it! The wince sounds like you are asking for permission.

- Leave ownership where it belongs with your boundary talks! When you feel uncomfortable with the communication, you may be tempted to compensate by *taking ownership* of the problem. Resist that temptation with all of your might! Again, using our roommate example, notice how the communication is undermined if I take ownership of your problem. "I am not looking for a roommate right now, but I can help you find someone who is." (What you really mean is, "Please, please don't be mad at me for saying no to this unreasonable and inappropriate request. I'll make it up to you by doing for you what you should be doing for yourself.") Remember, when you take ownership for the problem, you are leaving with an assignment. Do you really need another assignment?

Most of us can relate to sagging fences and broken boundaries. If we evaluate relationships that aren't working the way they should, we may find gaping holes in the wall or gates swinging in the wind. I encourage you to *walk your borders* and check your fences.

In the spirit of personal accountability, I also encourage you to self-assess. How might you be violating another's boundaries? We crash through boundaries when we:

1. Try to control or manipulate others (with guilt, fear, emotional withdrawal, or any other handy device).

2. Ask people to own what we are responsible for (otherwise known as low accountability or blame).

3. Get our needs met at the expense of others.

4. Take advantage of or exploit weakness in another person.

5. Fail to honor what another person values.

Is it possible that you are climbing over a fence without intending to or even realizing it?

When a colleague of mine asked herself that question, she realized for the first time she was indeed trespassing! "When I did the boundaries check, I found myself well over the line with my son and daughter-in-law. I was forever giving advice and involving myself in situations and decisions that belonged to them. They were stunned (and grateful) when I apologized and let them know that I would no longer be climbing over the fence. My relationship with both of them has improved so much—it is just remarkable."

In another example, a woman realized that she was violating boundaries by controlling and dominating conversation. "I made everything about me," she confesses now. "If you told a story, it reminded me of MY story, and I would interrupt your story to tell mine (because mine was so much more interesting)."

This woman was looking for validation. She was screaming to be heard and noticed and liked. To meet those needs, she crashed through boundaries. When she learned to validate others by listening and acknowledging them, she found the validation she had been looking for all along. "I listen more than I talk now," she smiles. "And I enjoy hearing another's story! My relationships are healthier, and I feel more at ease."

These are good examples of the difference boundaries can make in our relationships. The work starts on the inside with clear definition. It moves to the outside with effective communication. Every relationship in your life (including the one you have with yourself and the people you spend the most time with) will benefit from this process.

## JOURNALING EXERCISE

Take a moment to think about the fences in your life and relationships.

1. Are any of them broken or compromised?

2. How might the triple A model help in a situation you are facing right now? How would it sound if you were to use it?

3. Are you undermining a stand you are taking by apologizing for it?

4. Have you ever been tempted to compensate (or apologize) for a boundary by taking ownership of the problem?

5. In what ways could you be compromising or violating another's boundaries?

## 15

# FRAMING LIFE EVENTS

*Optimism is a skill*

HERE IS AN INTRIGUING question, posed by Wendy Edey, the director of counseling at the Hope Foundation of Alberta: "In your situation, where you find yourself right now—faced with the decisions you face—what would a hopeful person do?"[1]

What a wonderful question!

Think for a moment about your current condition or the problem weighing heavily on your heart. In this situation, what would a hopeful person say? What would a hopeful person *do*? Even if you are not feeling particularly hopeful just now, you can step back and view the situation through hopeful eyes.

Looking through other eyes is often a breakthrough strategy. An exercise we sometimes use with corporate clients is a stepping-out exercise. When the organization is faced with a complex issue, we invite them to step away from the problem and view it through other eyes. Not just any eyes...we pick innovative, risk-taking, on-the-edge-of-your seat eyes. These are eyes that will see your problem from a completely different perspective.

If you are in the medical industry, we might ask you to look at your problem through the eyes of Google or Amazon. If you're in the mortgage business, we might ask you to think like Starbucks or Apple. What would they do if faced with your issue?

Looking through hopeful eyes is a lot like this exercise. It invites you to step away from the problem, the decision, or the risk and see it as a hopeful person would. This is very effective, especially when you aren't feeling like a hopeful person.

*If you want to change the way you feel, you must change the way you think.*

Several years ago I was attacked in the hallway of a hotel and badly beaten while on a speaking tour through the South. That event changed everything. Up to that point I had been naïve, even cavalier about my personal safety. Honestly, I didn't give safety a second thought. Violence was something that happened to other people or on television dramas. In a moment, I went from being overly confident to insecure and frightened. I wondered if I would ever be the same.

I won't be. Not ever.

I will never be the "Dondi" I was before the attack. (And that, by the way, is a good thing.) The goal is not to rewind time; it is to turn every experience (no matter how painful or difficult) into a stepping-stone rather than a stumbling block.

It was a steep climb out of that valley, physically and emotionally, but my confidence has been restored. That event has served me well. I wouldn't trade it for anything, because I learned something very important, something beyond personal safety.

*I learned that events do not define you; they reveal you.*

Imagine for a moment that I am holding an orange. If I squeeze the orange with all of my might, what will come out? (Play along; there is a point.)

If you're thinking *juice*, you are right, but not just any kind of juice—not strawberry, raspberry, or grape juice. It will be orange juice. In fact, it will always be orange juice, no matter who squeezes the orange, no matter where they squeeze it or when. Why?

Because it's an orange!

Here's the point: we know that it will always be orange juice, because that is what's inside an orange. And here's how this relates to you and the way you frame life events. When life presses on you—when circumstances are crushing—whatever is inside of you will come out.

If hope and faith and resiliency come out of you in times like these, that's what is in there. If fear and anger and hopelessness come out, that's what is inside. The event didn't put it there! There is a very important principle at work here. Events show us what is already on the inside.

Through that experience, I realized something else. For years to that point, I had been reading, studying, absorbing, and teaching disciplines of success and personal effectiveness. These strategies were the tools of my trade, and I had internalized them. I am so thankful for that; if you had given me a book on optimism, confidence, or personal accountability after the attack, I might have been tempted to knock you right over the head with it!

I would not have been interested in learning coping strategies or developing personal resiliency. This was not a growing moment; it was a time for drawing from the well. Thank God, what I needed to recover was already firmly planted inside of me. When life pressed in, faith and hope and resiliency poured out.

The life's work of Dr. Martin Seligman teaches us that optimism is learned. Seligman draws on more than twenty years of clinical research to demonstrate how optimism enhances the quality of life and how anyone can learn to practice it.[2] I do think of optimism as a skill. Unfortunately, negativity appears to be automatic or more natural—it is easier to learn.

In the workplace, negativity is a pervasive problem—a battle many organizations are losing. Where there is negativity, you will find high turnover and absenteeism, an increase in employee grievances and complaints, a lack of trust, and generalized cynicism. From there, negativity will impact quality, efficiency, and customer service. If allowed, negativity will reach through the organization and literally push customers away!

In *Managing Workplace Negativity*, Gary Topchik gives us three factors that influence individual and company-wide negativity: "Negativity is often the result of a loss of confidence, control, or community."[3] In consulting with organizations and individuals, I have found this to be absolutely true. These three elements are critical, whether we are facing negativity in our personal or professional lives.

1. People with low self-esteem and confidence tend to be more critical of others and the organizations they work for. If I already feel pretty terrible about myself, admitting a mistake or taking personal responsibility might push me right over the edge! I look outside of myself to explain, defend, and rationalize. The only way I know how to make myself feel taller is by making others look smaller; I do that by locating faults and deficiencies in others. Over time, criticism becomes the lens I look through. It is habitual.

2. When people feel out of control, the natural reaction is to resist. Resistance looks a lot like negativity. In most organizations change is constant, rapid, and often disconnected. The workforce is change fatigued. There is often a generalized sense that employees can't impact what they are responsible for (and tomorrow there will be another new program and another new priority).

3. People long to belong. We want to feel connected and valued. We want to be part of something worthwhile—something with strong purpose. When these attributes are not present, we become disillusioned, and we disengage. Negativity is a natural by-product of feeling isolated or *uninvited*. Sadly, this can happen in the workplace and at home.

My advice to organizations battling negativity is pretty straightforward:

1. *Focus on building the confidence and self-esteem of your workforce.* Everything you do to raise confidence will positively impact the bottom line—from attendance to turnover to productivity. Create more opportunities for success, celebrate victories, and authentically demonstrate value for people. Build skill, trust people with meaningful assignments, and communicate absolute faith in their ability to perform.

2. *Give people a greater sense of control!* Push decisions to the level most impacted by them whenever you can. This won't always be possible, of course. (When my son was two years old and getting ready to step out into the middle of a busy intersection, I didn't stand by and say, "Oh, he's going to learn from that." I pulled his two-year-old behind back up on the curb! That was not a decision I could allow him to make. Still, there are lots of decisions a two-year-old can make. And that is true for every person at any age.) Whenever you can, let the person who must live with the decision make it.

3. *Finally, focus on building the team and a strong sense of community.* Knock down the barriers between functions and divisions. Encourage and reward collaborative efforts. Design interdependence with a shared vision. Make sure everyone understands the impact they can have, and invite everyone to the party!

Ultimately, we are in charge of how we respond to the events of life. We may not control what happens, but we always control how we respond to what happens. This is where *framing* sets the stage. How we frame or interpret an event will always determine our response to it.

We know that pessimists see events as permanent, pervasive, and blameworthy! Pessimists are famous for absolute language. *Everything* is ruined! *Everyone* is upset! *No one* cares about me. Pessimists are also past-oriented. They focus on what happened or didn't happen. And the pessimist's ultimate goal is to assign responsibility (or blame). Sometimes they blame themselves, and sometimes they blame others.

Optimists see things differently. Setbacks are temporary, isolated events and solvable. They have a future focus; less concerned with what happened, they look ahead to options, solutions, and action. Optimists are not interested in fixing blame. They want to fix the problem. Blame is irrelevant.[4]

With those definitions, you can see how a pessimist and an optimist can look at the same set of circumstances and see very different things. That is the power of framing. Consider this example. A woman's husband has declined her invitation to attend a community play. Listen to the difference the frame makes:

- "He refused to go *last time* too. He *never* supports me in *anything* I want to do. *He makes me feel* so unwanted and alone."

- "There are many things we enjoy doing together, and *this* is not one of them. The play is important to me, and I *choose* to go. *Next week* we will plan an evening together, doing something both of us look forward to."

The greatest difference between these responses probably isn't the frame; it is the impact on the relationship. The first response blows the situation up and makes it about *everything*. (This is no longer about a play; it is complete and utter disappointment in another human being.)

This woman reaches into history and dredges up past disappointments. Absolute language abounds with words like *never* and *anything*. She gives her personal power away by abdicating responsibility for how she feels. Before you know it, this woman will convince herself that her husband has never done anything right, the relationship is a mess, and she has married the wrong guy!

The second response isolates the issue and makes it about the play, not the person. Blame and judgment are removed and solutions are applied. This woman empowers herself by owning her choices, and she reaches into the future with a plan.

In these two scenarios we see once again how words shape outcomes. We set the course by the way we talk about events. Optimistic or hopeful thinking opens the door to problem solving, exploring options, and creativity. It allows us to look past what *is* to what *can be*. It builds relationships and empowers people with choices. Optimism is disarming. In the absence of blame, people lose the need to defend, excuse, or rationalize.

Just as optimism is a skill and can be learned, negativity is a habit. It is simply unchecked pessimism. If you find yourself framing events as a pessimist would, you can do something about that. You can begin looking at life through the eyes of an optimist—through hopeful eyes. When you change the frame, you change the response. When you change the response, you change the outcome.

## JOURNALING EXERCISE

Practice optimism with these reflective exercises:

1. On a scale from 1 to 10, with 1 a pessimistic view, where do you see yourself now?

2. How do your beliefs impact your frames? What needs to change?

3. Think about a difficult situation you are facing now. How would a hopeful person frame it? What would a hopeful person do in this situation?

## 16

# GRACE AND GRATITUDE NOURISH HOPE

*Gratitude encourages the heart*

YEARS AGO I HAD the opportunity to travel through South Africa on a speaking tour. On this trip I learned the most beautiful lessons in gratitude. Without exception, the auditoriums were filled with thousands of people. Many of them had never attended a professional conference, and they were genuinely grateful for the opportunity.

They did not mind standing when the seats were filled. They did not worry if we ran short on handouts. They did not even seem to notice if the room was too hot or too cold. They were happy to be there—it was a great privilege to attend!

Throughout the trip I watched people work, and they did it with such joy. Once I caught the hotel housekeeping staff singing and dancing on a break! When I turned the corner, they stopped immediately and apologized profusely. I laughed and begged them to continue! (It was absolutely refreshing, and I joined them.)

I watched families dance all the way to church on a Sunday morning; late that afternoon I heard them laughing and singing on their way home. I rushed to the window to watch their return. They had traveled miles each way—dancing and singing like that, and they did not look weary at all. They looked young and happy and full of life. I admired them.

Along the way I learned that many of the people who would make my stay comfortable and safe were living in cardboard homes with no electricity or running water. Fire was a great danger, as they used candles to light paper houses. Even so, they appeared each day bright and clean, pressed and professional.

There was such a grace about these people—a graciousness that was disarming and refreshing. I fell in love with them! They were unspoiled and grateful for the simple, beautiful pleasures of life. As the plane took off to carry me home, I knew I would miss Africa. I was grateful for what it had shown me, and I knew I would return someday.

Back in the States at my first speaking engagement, the first words I heard as I stepped into the banquet room were, "The parking in this place is ridiculous." I cringed! This wasn't new, but I was seeing it through new eyes. I include myself in this observation: we are spoiled. We forget to be grateful and how to marvel at what is simple and precious. We let foolish things annoy us, and we give our strength to things that should not even get our attention.

*Gratitude is a powerful thing. It produces resiliency and hope. Gratitude encourages the heart. Gratitude heals.*

Research draws a direct line between gratitude and health, and the body of evidence continues to grow.

> Given that expressions of praise and thanksgiving are key components of religious worship, the physiological effects of gratitude hold promise for understanding religion's impact on health, perhaps even as a mediator of the robust association between religiousness and physical health.[1]

"There are some very interesting studies linking optimism to better immune function," says Lisa Aspinwall, PhD, a psychology professor at the University of Utah.[2]

> Research suggests that grateful people have more energy and optimism, are less bothered by life's hassles, are more resilient in the face of stress, have better health, and suffer less depression than the rest of us. People who practice gratitude—and

yes, it is something one can learn and improve—are also more compassionate, more likely to help others, less materialistic, and more satisfied with life.[3]

To fully appreciate the power of gratitude, we might also look at the other end of the spectrum. The absence or lack of gratitude leaves a mark on performance, morale, and most certainly the bottom line. A simple thank-you is one of the most powerful forms of recognition available, and it costs nothing! The absence of gratitude, on the other hand, can be very, very expensive.

- According to a Gallup poll, 65 percent of workers say they didn't receive a single word of praise or recognition in the past year.[4]

- Companies that effectively value and appreciate employees enjoy more than triple returns on equity and assets, and they achieve higher operating margins than companies that do not.[5]

- An estimated 22 million workers are presently "actively disengaged," or extremely negative in their workplace. This costs the U.S. economy up to $300 billion dollars a year in productivity—undoubtedly an underestimate because it does not account for absence, illness, and other problems that result when workers are disengaged from their work and their companies.[6]

- The U.S. Department of Labor credits lack of appreciation as the number one reason employees quit.[7]

- *TIME* magazine tallied the "Cost of Incivility" in a February 2005 article. Citing a management journal, the article reports almost 80 percent of employees

do not feel respected at work, and 60 percent think
it's getting worse. This report went on to say that one
in eight employees who are treated rudely will leave,
and the average Fortune 1000 executive spends about
13 percent (or seven weeks a year) of his or her time
handling employee disputes. (Ouch, do that math!)[8]

Leaders who get this one right...win. Here is a classy example of
leadership engaging employees through authentic appreciation.

The employees of a large consulting firm worked around the clock
for more than six months to meet the requirements of a complex
project. Fourteen-hour days were not uncommon, and work-life
balance was a myth. "It was definitely an all-work-and-no-play situation," remembers one employee. But that isn't the end of her story or
what she remembers and talks about the most. This is the story of a
leader who got it right.

The project was successfully completed just before the holidays. We were all exhausted and burned out. Normally the
company hosted an extravagant, employee-only awards
dinner to celebrate the holidays and recognize outstanding
performance. This year nothing had been mentioned about
that tradition. We just assumed it wasn't a priority with so
much going on, and to tell you the truth, most of us were
relieved. That would have been one more dinner we didn't
share with our families, and our personal lives were stretched
a little thin.

The CEO hadn't forgotten about the annual dinner or the recognition. He had another plan. Beautiful baskets filled with gourmet
treats were delivered to every employee at home. On the card was
written, "Thank you for your extraordinary commitment. This gift
comes with our deepest appreciation for you and for the people who

support your efforts from home. Families are not on the payroll, but they are on the team."

This gesture was meaningful and successful on several levels. The employees were tired, and leadership understood dinner out wasn't the best way to say thank you. They realized the strain fourteen-hour days have on relationships, and they acknowledged the people behind the scenes.[9]

I love to see organizations get it right, and many of them do. I also see many of them get it very wrong! A top performer who left his company after more than a decade of service had this to say:

> Things are not perfect in my new situation. We have many of the same issues and frustrations I experienced with my last company. The big difference is simple. My new leader acknowledges what isn't working and partners with me to solve problems. I believe she understands what I am going through and authentically cares. I feel appreciated and valued. That changes everything. I am optimistic about my future here.

Appreciation (or the lack of) will ultimately touch the customer. When asked to help organizations improve customer satisfaction, my first question is, "How high is employee satisfaction?" There is a direct connection between these two elements. Happy employees make happy customers. Miserable employees make miserable customers (and at some level actually enjoy doing it).

If an organization wants to increase customer loyalty, my first recommendation is this: treat your employees exactly as you want them to treat your finest customers. That's not rocket science, but I am amazed at how often organizations miss the mark.

The impact of genuine gratitude—the spirit of thankfulness—is compelling. There is no doubt about the impact appreciation has on relationships and results. It changes everything!

I invite you to personally test the power of gratitude in your own life. Here are eleven ways you can nourish hope and develop a positive expectancy—in yourself and in others. I encourage you to do these things even when you don't feel like it—better yet, *especially* when you don't feel like it—because gratitude really does have a way of changing everything...beginning with how you feel.

1. *Start with gratitude every day.* Before your feet hit the floor in the morning, find three things to be thankful for. Express your gratitude aloud, with real feeling. (If this feels ridiculous, maybe it will make you laugh, and I can think of worse ways to start the day.)

2. *Recognize and talk about what you value in others.* Everyone responds to feeling valued and valuable. In management school we learn "what gets recognized gets repeated." When you recognize value...you get more.

3. *Put positive information in.* We are bombarded every day with negative news and cynical perspectives. It's difficult to walk around in all of that without some of it rubbing off on us. Counter negativity by exposing yourself to positive, uplifting messages. Negativity will make you weak and sick. Immunize yourself.

4. *Teach your children the power of gratitude.* This goes way beyond reminding them to say, "Thank you." Gratitude is not a debt to be paid or an obligation to be polite. It is allowing what is good and right in the world to sink in to our bones. It is enjoying the moment we are in. It is noticing what is beautiful. We may express gratitude with words, but gratitude itself is an emotion.

5. *Develop the discipline of gratitude* (otherwise known as fake it until you make it). Tell your face to be happy; your mind and heart will try to follow. It is absolutely impossible to be grateful and grumpy at the same time. I'm telling you, it cannot be done! Sometimes I test this theory with a live audience. I will ask them to sit up, smile broadly, and try to say, "I don't want to be here." It doesn't work! Even though the words are negative, the message sounds alive and happy—happy to be here! Likewise, if I ask them to slump in their chairs, frown, and say, "I'm so glad I came," it doesn't have a ring of truth. The words fall flat on the floor (right next to the energy).

6. *Stop looking for what is wrong!* Start looking for and talking about what is right with the world. Before critiquing or evaluating, look for what is good in every person and every situation. I dare you to try this for one week. (This is harder than it sounds, by the way.) After this weeklong experiment, you can decide if you want to continue. I'm betting you will. Life is brighter and more beautiful when you view it through grateful eyes.

7. *Find the positive intention.* Even really *stupid* behavior has an intention. If you look behind the behavior (that is driving you crazy), you will often find a positive intention or an unmet need. (People do ridiculous things to get their needs met.) Focus on the need or the intention, and quite often the crazy behavior will take care of itself.

8. *Make an appointment with gratitude.* If you've been keeping your appointments with worry, perhaps you can add gratitude to the agenda. After you've worried yourself sufficiently, take five minutes to recall everything you are grateful for.

9. *Put appreciation on your to-do list.* If it is true that 65 percent of us haven't been thanked this year, perhaps you can do something about that. By the way, appreciation is not reserved for supervisors and managers. We all have the power to change that horrifying statistic, one thank-you at a time.

10. *Search out the silent heroes in your life.* These are the people who quietly make it happen. They won't blow their own horns, and they are often overlooked. Make sure that doesn't happen in your house or your office!

11. *Encourage the people who have encouraged you.* Make a list of the people you are grateful for and why. Then go out of your way to let them know how much you appreciate them. You may never realize how perfect your timing is. Just when they need it the most—just when they aren't feeling valued or valuable—along you come with a message of gratitude.

## JOURNALING EXERCISE

1. Keep a running list of what and whom you are grateful for.

2. How have gratitude and appreciation inspired you in the past?

3. What are you giving your strength to that should not be getting your attention?

4. Who are the silent heroes in your life? How can you demonstrate a greater appreciation for who they are, what they do, and the difference they make?

5. As you implement gratitude *strategies*, what are you noticing? How is gratitude impacting your relationships and results?

## REFLECTIONS

## PART II: SEEDS OF HOPE

The list below will help you to internalize the principles from part 2 of this book and will give you direction for the actions you can take to sow seeds of hope and expectancy in the midst of adverse circumstances. Remember that the pain you may be feeling, the struggles you are in, and the disappointments you have experienced can become seeds of hope and expectancy for a bright and blessing-filled future.

## DISCOVERING THE SEEDS OF HOPE AND EXPECTANCY

- Just as words can build and empower, they are able to cripple and destroy. Be careful what you say to yourself and others because the words you speak are the seeds you are planting in their lives. Whatever is in the seed will grow. It will produce.

- Replace what is negative and limiting with what is positive and empowering. This is a process in which something must stop (the negativity) and something must start (positive, powerful proclamations).

- Seeds can only produce what they are. Seeds of faith produce faith. Seeds of discouragement produce discouragement.

- The story you tell about your future is like a road map. An old map will take you to an old place. If you want to move beyond the old boundaries, you must create a new map with a new story.

- Many people have worthy, even exciting aspirations. Only a small percentage of people actually put these in writing and consistently read them. The moment you take these steps, you have separated yourself from the multitude that stops with a dream. You give your dream strong legs to run on.

- Progress produces hope. When you see yourself moving closer to the goal, you get your second and third wind! Make your progress visible. Set your stones.

- Ultimately you will answer the question: "What do I value most?" You answer by the choices you make. Your time, actions, and energy should reflect what you value. If they don't, something must change—either you must change your focus or become more honest about what you really value.

- There will be times when you acquire balance through rest. Allow yourself these seasons; they have tremendous purpose in your life. Seeds know about seasons; inside of each one the potential waits to burst forth at just the right moment.

- Effective boundaries allow you to live, love, and work productively. They guard your self-respect, protect what you value, and allow you to ask for what you need. Without proper boundaries, personal and professional relationships are jeopardized.

- "In your situation, where you find yourself right now—faced with the decisions you face—what would a hopeful person do?"[10]

- If you want to change the way you feel, you must change the way you think.

- Events do not define you; they reveal you.

- Ultimately, you are in charge of how you respond to the events of life. You may not control what happens, but you always control how you respond to what happens. This is where *framing* sets the stage. How you frame or interpret an event will always determine your response to it.

- Gratitude is a powerful thing. It produces resiliency and hope. Gratitude encourages the heart. Gratitude heals.

*Part III*

# PRODUCING

# RELEASING THE POTENTIAL WITHIN

*The flowers have already appeared in the land;*
*The time has arrived for pruning the vines,*
*And the voice of the turtledove has been heard in our land.*
—SONG OF SOLOMON 2:12, NAS

I MAGINE A VINE DESIGNED to climb with nothing to hold to or reach for. Even so, the vine is also designed to grow, and it will try. Without support, growth will be low; what should be climbing and reaching will simply creep along the ground. There is no structure or shape to it. If this vine bears fruit, it will lie on the ground hidden from sight. When fruit lies on the ground, it is likely to rot!

However, when tied to a trellis, that same vine, which has been designed to grow and climb, will do both of these things beautifully. The potential for that is in the seed, and we have already learned that whatever seeds *are* they become. The vine will reach up and through the trellis, supported and trained by the structure it clings to. With pruning, the branches become stronger, and in due season this vine will bear beautiful, healthy fruit.

The metaphor of a trellis serves us well. With this image we can explore the process of growing into our dreams with structure, training, and support. These three elements will allow you to stretch successfully and systematically out of your comfort zone and into your vision of the future.

1. The frame of a trellis provides structured growth. If you've been following along with the journaling exercises, much of this framework is already in place. Your grand design includes the goals you have set, the boundaries you have established, and the beliefs you have cultivated. We'll work on another piece of the framework now. It is your current reality—where you are today. When you hold your current story up to the one you want to write, the gaps will show. You can fill them with skills, experiences, and knowledge.

2. Pruning is purposefully cutting away what does not work and training the vine to follow the frame. Here you shape growth with feedback, personal development, and a *personal balance sheet* of skills and abilities you own and the ones you want to add.

3. Support will come from growing your network and seeking mentors. These external resources stabilize and promote growth. Like tying the vine to a trellis, we connect with these external resources to stabilize and promote growth.

We began with clearing the ground—pulling out of our lives what hinders growth. Next we explored what must be planted in our lives to live with expectancy. Now we will look at perennial hope. We have discovered what produces hope. Now we will see what hope can produce in us and in others.

# 17

# REACH BEYOND YOUR COMFORT ZONE

*To have more or become more,*
*I will have to do new things*

HOW OFTEN DO WE seek security over opportunity? Author Brian Tracy has said, "The more you seek security, the less of it you have. But the more you seek opportunity, the more likely it is that you will achieve the security that you desire."[1]

When we are called to something wonderful and awesome, do we shrink from it, thinking, "Who am I to do this marvelous thing?" What if we asked instead, "Why not me?" or "Who but me!"

The space between where you are today and where you want to be could be named *Growth*. It might also be called *Risk*! Unfortunately for some, it is known as *Impossible* or *Fear*. For a large number of people this space is simply *Unknown*. They would ask, "What gap?"

What should be grafted into this space is an action plan, like a puzzle piece cut to fill the space perfectly. It is the trellis we must build to encourage and support our *climb*.

The stretch between your current reality and your possibility may be very uncomfortable, if not a bit frightening. That's why instead of reaching beyond ourselves and doing what we need to improve, we often end up practicing what we are good at now. We do more of what has worked before or what we know. Our comfort zone calls us back to what is familiar, and from there we cannot hear the call of what is next!

Like old maps and old stories, continually doing what we have always done will bring us back to old places, the places we have been before. Repeat after me: *What got me here will not take me one step further. To have more or become more, I will have to do new things.*

Keep in mind that this is not just about careers. This applies to any of your goals. Here are a few examples of stories I've collected along the way:

- After retiring last year, Sharon pictured herself relaxing and enjoying long lazy days. "Three months into that, I was over it," she laughs. "The days are long all right, but this is not how I want to spend the best years of my life. My job is finished, but my work is not done. I want to make a difference in my community."

- A woman writes to say, "I work for a great company, but I have a bigger vision for the work and for myself. I want to do more with my life, and I'm not sure that is possible here."

- A young mother feels pushed and pulled by her current reality: "My story isn't working very well. We have a three-year-old, and my job is taking too much away from being the mother I want to be. We need the income, but I am going to have to find a better way. Something has to change."

- Many of us can probably relate to this realization: "My career started before I was finished with school. A part-time job in college morphed into a full-time position. I didn't intend to stay here for twelve years, but I here I am. This isn't the career I planned for myself. I'm not even using my education! Switching tracks at this point in my life just feels a little risky. I know I am

settling—exchanging my dreams and satisfaction for
what is comfortable and *easy*."

- Beth dreams of owning her own business. For several
  years she has been researching opportunities and
  reading entrepreneurial literature. She has done the
  market research, developed a compelling business
  plan, and secured financing. What keeps her from
  taking the next step? Beth is afraid of failing. (And she
  is surrounded by people who are happy to remind her
  that most new businesses fail within the first year.)

All of these stories have a common theme. There is a dream on the
inside—a new story waiting and wanting to unfold. They have something else in common. The road they are traveling probably won't
take them where they dream of going. But what does that have to do
with hope?

*Hope flourishes when we are fully invested in what we love—what
we are passionate about—and when we are growing and making a
real difference. Hope grows when we build on our natural strengths
and talents—when we honor our gifts and grow with the grain.*

## Map Your Route and Build Your Road

When it comes to career plans, many of the people I meet don't really
have one. One of the most frequent questions I am asked is: "How do
I pull together a plan for my career?"

Julie, a dynamic executive in the Silicon Valley, shared a powerful
insight at a mentoring event: "As I look around this organization, I
know one of the greatest differences between me and the people who
aren't on the executive team is a real plan. I have always had one, and
it has served me well."

While we may look to our employer for direction, organizations
often struggle to provide career maps. Many leaders tell me that

*dead ends* are real issues within the organization. "It is very diffi-cult to motivate people when there really is nowhere else for them to go," managers confide. This is a serious retention problem, because talented people want to see the road ahead. When people cannot see a future for themselves where they work, the organization risks losing them.

Before we go any further, please understand there is no such thing as a dead end for you—not in your career or in any goal you may set for yourself!

In some organizations, vertical moves are limited. If that is true for you, your challenge is to develop a broader set of skills and expe-riences from your current position. You may even find it necessary to move *over* or *out* of your current situation to reach your goals. It may look like there is a stop sign in front of you just now, but it is not a dead end you are facing—it is a turning point!

In my experience, career-pathing exercises (even if the organiza-tion has a formal process) are only as strong as the organization's commitment to professional development, coaching, and mentoring. The problem is that one size does not fit all. *Organizations can provide a chart, but they cannot chart the course.* Paths are personal things. Each is unique, just as unique as the person who travels them. So we shouldn't wait for someone to roll out the corporate rug. It is up to us to build our own road.

Often the approach to career planning begins with questions like: "What did you want to be when you grew up?" "Where do you see yourself in five years?" The answer may be a blank stare. Perhaps we should have these answers, but sometimes we don't. Maybe there is a better way to find your path. We'll start with your current story, the one you already have.

At the beginning of this book, you gathered your beliefs, thought about your story, and tried to capture its theme. In chapter 11, "Grand Designs," you spent some time writing the story of your future. Let's look specifically at your career goals and compare where you hope to be in the future with where you are right now. If we hold up the current situation to your dream of the future, the gaps will shine through.

- What is your job like?

- What do you love about it? What do you dread about it?

- What attracted you to it in the first place?

- What do you most look forward to? (If you just answered, "Friday," please try again.)

- What are your gifts and talents—what comes naturally for you? What is effortless for you? What are you doing when you are *in your zone?*

When Teresa considered questions like these, she answered:

My job is like a well-worn suit. At one time it was top of the line. I worked hard to earn it, and it fit well. I have grown, and the suit hasn't. It isn't comfortable anymore. It constricts and confines. It's a little threadbare and outdated. I was attracted to this job (and this company) for the creativity and challenge it offered. We were growing and innovating. Now my department is in more of a maintenance mode, and my work is less exciting. I am an innovator and a risk-taker. I love the challenge of a complex problem or a new opportunity. When I am in my "zone," I am collaborating with others and designing solutions. I am good at blending ideas and selling the benefits of change.

With this as a starting point, Teresa began to isolate the gaps between where she was and where she wanted to be in the future. These included financial, position, responsibility, authority, and scope of work gaps. She studied the organization and looked for opportunities to be on the leading edge of change.

Gaps may also be perceptions—this is your reputation or brand. It is how others see you and what they believe about you and your capabilities. It is what they think of when your name is mentioned and the words they use to describe you.

Perceptions are operating around us all of the time. Some of these are positive and open doors of opportunity. Others block the path. Like an invisible wall we bang into, we aren't quite sure what just happened, but we know we were *knocked back*.

Perceptions can be neutral—like giant question marks next to our name. These are things people don't know about us and words they wouldn't use to describe us. We need to pay attention to these as well, because neutral perceptions may include things you want people to understand about you. Neutral could mean positive impressions aren't getting through or aren't reaching your intended audience.

Whether we realize it or not, neutral or negative perceptions have limited all of us. In her search, Teresa located a significant perception gap. "I thought of myself as very strategic, proactive, and creative, but my manager didn't use words like that to describe my strengths. She talked about my dependability, reliability, and thoroughness. When she finished, I felt like she might be talking about a workhorse on the farm."

Dependability, reliability, and thoroughness are certainly positive impressions, but they may not throw open the same doors as impressions like strategic, proactive, and visionary. As Teresa learned, the adjectives people used to describe her were also written on the doors opening to her. If she wanted to unlock a different door, she had to invite new, more powerful impressions. She also found huge question marks next to her name! Key people within the organization didn't know her or her work. "My network gap was more like a gaping hole," she realized.

Gaps will also include expectations. What will be expected of you in your future place? Ultimately, you will fill the gaps with knowledge, meaningful experiences, skills, a strong network, and a solid marketing plan.

Teresa found that most of her experiences were one-dimensional. "I had a deep understanding of my job but a very shallow and narrow understanding of the organization overall," she realized. "There were many exciting opportunities within the company, but I wasn't considered for those because I hadn't set and communicated my goals. I didn't understand the difference I could really make (so I shouldn't be surprised when others didn't make those connections). Really, I wasn't putting myself out there. I was passive about my job, and that made it less satisfying and less rewarding on many levels."

We cannot wait for a career plan to knock us over the head! Your organization may have resources for career planning (take full advantage of those), but ultimately you are in charge of developing and implementing a plan for your life. Here are seven strategies that may help you chart your path and start moving in the right direction:

1. *Study the paths of people who have gone before you.* You may not replicate their journey precisely, but you can create a sketch and work from there to adjust your path. A wonderful resource for studying career pilgrimage is Sheila Wellington's book *Be Your Own Mentor: Strategies from Top Women in the Secrets of Success.*[2]

2. *Interview people who are doing what you dream of.* What steps did they take? What obstacles did they encounter on the path? What have they learned along the way? What are the essential skills? What would they do differently if they were starting again?

3. *Focus on experiences versus promotions.* This is a little like focusing on the actions you can control and trusting results to take care of themselves. Rather than focusing your attention on the promotion you want, focus on the experiences you need to prepare for that position. Look for opportunities to practice and demonstrate the skills you will need.

4. *Think about and talk about skills that are transportable.* Find new ways to showcase your strengths. You will take abilities and experiences with you when you step into a new role. A retail sales associate, for example, can build a more compelling résumé by highlighting the skills that have prepared her for a management position. These might include negotiating, problem solving, communication, and so on. She will apply these skills differently and use them in a new context, but they will certainly go with her!

5. *Broaden your perspective.* The higher you climb within your field or organization, the more perspective you must have. This means you must have the ability to look across the organization rather than just up. When you develop a wider view of how the work is done, what the challenges are, and how the pieces fit together, you can be more strategic in your approach. You can acquire perspective by looking for opportunities to serve on cross-functional teams, special projects, or even volunteering for temporary assignments.

6. *Treat your plan like a work in progress.* This is not a document set in stone. It is a journey. Even with a map

in your hand, the itinerary may change as you travel. Along the way you may take an intentional detour to bridge a gap, pick up an experience, or strengthen your knowledge base. Down the road you may even decide to change the destination altogether. That doesn't mean the trip to this point has been irrelevant! Quite the opposite is true. The journey itself has made the new destination even more possible.

7. *Find your themes and grow with your grain.* In the best-selling book *Now Discover Your Strengths*, authors Buckingham and Clifton encourage us to build our lives around our strengths and talents. Too many of us "become experts in our weaknesses and spend our lives trying to repair these flaws."[3] Growing with your grain simply means that you have identified the strengths that are built into you. You came with these, like batteries included. They are the *raw materials*. When you add knowledge and skills, the raw materials become the product you can market and sell.

For some, success is measured by the ability to move up or forward. For others, it may be the opportunity to make a bigger difference, develop a specialized skill, or be recognized as the expert in a particular field. Success may simply be doing what you love the most, or it can be all of the above!

Paths, indeed, are personal things, and they don't just magically *appear*. We can certainly take advantage of the resources available to us and learn from those who have gone before. Ultimately, each of us has the opportunity to carve out a path that is as unique as we are.

## JOURNALING EXERCISES

1. What have you been seeking more of, security or opportunity?

2. What are the themes of your current story? What is your job like? (Be creative here. Pull in what is positive and negative about your current situation. Experiment with a metaphor, like Teresa's suit.)

3. What do you see when you hold the current story up to the one you would like to write?

4. How does your present situation allow you to use and showcase your gifts?

5. What are your *raw materials?*

6. What skills do you need to add to your raw materials to make yourself more marketable?

## 18

# TRAINING THE VINE

*When it comes to garden stakes and*
*clippers, think feedback*

THERE IS A PARADOX in every beautiful garden. Cutting back or pruning strengthens, promotes growth, and encourages plants to bloom. As it turns out, these are just a few of the benefits.

Pruning lets in light and air. It removes what is damaged and highlights the best features of a plant. It rejuvenates old plants or those that have been neglected. It can change the direction of growth or inspire growth in a new area. It controls pests and helps plants fit into difficult or tight spaces. (Pruning ensures that plants don't invade the space of others. Sounds like another lesson in boundaries!)

What a wonderful metaphor for growing people! While the process of cutting away what doesn't work or what is limiting our growth may be uncomfortable, it is clearly profitable. I love the idea of letting more air and light into my life, removing what is damaged, and showcasing my best features! Most of us have at one time or another needed help in a difficult place or space. And *rejuvenation*? Bring it on! Even the definition gets my attention: to make young again; "to restore to a former state; make fresh or new again."

When it comes to garden stakes and clippers, think feedback. Feedback is one of the most effective tools available to you. Use it to reinforce what is working and to *cut away* what is not. The call to action here is continuous improvement. It is taking feedback, whether spoken or silent, and putting it to work for you—making it profitable.

What have you learned and implemented in the last thirty days based on feedback? When I ask that question, even in large audiences only a few people can honestly answer. The majority of the people I speak with are waiting for feedback to knock on their door. When it does, they crack open the door slowly and invite feedback in very cautiously (or begrudgingly), like an unwelcome guest to dinner.

Sometimes feedback feels like a slap in the face. (Believe me, I've been there. There are days when I feel like I've received more feedback than any human deserves in a lifetime.) When that happens, we may feel like slamming the door on this rude, ungrateful guest! Or perhaps we go to the other extreme. We change feedback into a weapon and beat ourselves silly with it. We turn the feedback over and over in our mind and learn the wrong lesson from it. Denying feedback or brutalizing ourselves with it is (at the very least) unproductive.

For a life trying to grow, feedback is essential; it is one of the tools we use to train our growth. We leverage feedback when we learn to do two things well—first, know where to find it, and second, know how to process it effectively.

Honestly, feedback is all around us. It is in what people say or don't say, in the assignments we receive (or don't), in how others respond to us, and, ultimately, in the results we achieve. Some of the most profitable feedback can be found in what is frustrating you right now! When we don't get the support we need or the response we expected, that is feedback. When something isn't working the way it should, we are getting feedback.

If you are fortunate, you work for and with people who know how to give and receive feedback in a healthy and constructive way. The dialogue is open, honest, and designed to help people grow. But what if that does not describe your situation?

*When it comes to feedback, we are wise to remember that people give us what they have, not necessarily what we need.*

You may have to *coach* the coach to get your feedback or to make the feedback you are getting more useful. That was the case for Connie.

Connie's feedback generally happened once each year with her performance review. Typically, the conversation was shallow and strained. "My manager was extremely nervous, and that made me nervous," she laughs. "It was so awkward. I would leave the meeting not quite sure how I was doing or what I could be doing differently. Sometimes I left thinking a giant elephant had been in the room, but neither of us wanted to talk about it."

That's when Connie decided to coach the coach. "I flipped the process over completely," she told me. "I asked my manager the questions I needed her to ask of me. For example, she wasn't thinking about how I could become more valuable to the organization, so I asked her that question. I also asked her to think about my future with the organization—what I could be doing to prepare for my next steps."

Asking strategic questions put Connie in the driver's seat with her feedback. "It definitely changed the scope of our conversations," Connie says as she smiles broadly. "The questions I asked required my manager to think about me differently. At first, she didn't have solid input for me, but over time the quality of the feedback improved."

We'd like to think that people in management positions know how to give quality feedback. Unfortunately, that is not always true. Some managers are terrible at it or, at the very least, uncomfortable with it. We can't afford to wait for them to figure it out.

Realizing that her manager was uncomfortable providing feedback was also an important clue for Connie. "I made it very safe for her to share her opinions and perspectives with me. Instead of waiting for her to break the ice, I did that for both of us."

Connie's process is actually brilliant. She found a way to manage her manager and her feedback. If you recognize Connie's predicament, here is an outline of the steps she took to take control:

1. Ask strategic questions about how you can create more value in your current role and prepare for the future. ("What do you see as my greatest strengths, and how can I use them more often and more effectively?")

2. Ask the questions you wish your coach were asking! ("What do you see as a next, natural step for me, and how can I prepare to take that step?")

3. Find ways to open the dialogue and make feedback a more natural part of day-to-day communications. ("I want to make sure I am focusing on the top priorities. How can I have more of an impact on what is truly important?")

As in Connie's case, getting quality feedback is the first step. How you process the *data* is also critical. Feedback can build and strengthen you, or it can tear you up and tear you down. Here are seven things to keep in mind as you seek out and process feedback:

1. *Separate yourself from the feedback.* Depersonalize it. Remember, feedback is perception. It does not define who you are or what you are capable of. It simply reveals an impression. That's a good thing, because impressions revealed can be managed. Consider the alternative. When it comes to feedback, ignorance is not bliss. What you don't know can hurt you or, at the very least, hold you back.

2. *Seek to understand the feedback.* Whether you agree or disagree with the feedback you are receiving, make it your goal to understand. Resist every temptation to explain or justify. Instead, ask questions to

clarify. Remember, agreement is not the goal. Understanding is.

3. *Isolate the parts you can control.* There may be things inside of feedback you cannot personally control. Acknowledge these, and focus your energy and responses on the things you can do something about.

4. *Share your action plan.* Honor feedback by letting people know what you plan to do with it. This may be as simple as, "I appreciate your perspective on this, and I will keep it in mind." Or it may be a list of action items you plan to implement.

5. *Take a break!* If the feedback is particularly difficult or delivered in an awkward or ineffective way, you may need to step back. Have your script ready! You can say, "You've certainly given me something to think about. I'd like to do that before we discuss it further."

6. *Get a second opinion!* If you receive feedback that is difficult to accept or out-of-the-ballpark different from feedback you've received in the past, consult a mentor. Ask for some help in processing the data to understand what it means and how to manage it productively.

7. *Look for clues about what is important.* The feedback you receive tells you what is important to others—what they value. When you know what people value, you are in a better position to increase your value to them! At the very least, you will understand how to manage their expectations in the future. In this light, even negative feedback is a win. (It won't feel like you are

winning when you receive it. Trust the process, and review items 1–6.)

A *personal balance sheet* will assist you in processing and managing feedback.[1] The balance sheet works on the premise that you have value and you have the ability to increase your personal value. It allows you to plan, mark, and promote your growth.

| Strengths/ Abilities | Emerging Strengths | Areas of Development |
|---|---|---|
|  |  |  |
|  |  |  |
|  |  |  |

In the strengths column, list your abilities and areas of expertise. These are the skills and knowledge areas you own and are known for. Emerging strengths are things you are working on; for example, you are practicing and increasing your confidence; you are close to the tipping point and beginning to hit your stride. The development areas are your gaps. You need to add these to abilities in order to achieve your goals.

As you build your balance sheet, refer to the beliefs you captured and cataloged when we started. How are those reflected here? Pull out your goals, and have a conversation with a coach or mentor. In reviewing the balance sheet, here are a few things you may want to think about:

1. Are your strengths known to you and to others?

2. How are you measuring progress on the emerging strengths? Is your progress visible to others?

3. What is the most important area of development now?

4. How can you design opportunities to develop in those areas?

The balance sheet is an ongoing and dynamic process of addition. When you master an emerging strength, it shifts to the strengths column. As your goals come into focus and you process feedback, you will identify areas needing more attention or development. Each time you add an ability or strength, you increase your value. You reduce the gaps and create opportunity.

## REFLECTING POOLS: THE POWER OF PERSONAL REFLECTION

In our journey together, you have spent time reflecting on what you believe about you. What others believe about you is also reflected there, because our beliefs are shaped to some degree by the messages we receive (and accept) from others. While we want to be open and available for those impressions and perceptions, we cannot afford to lose ourselves in feedback. Center yourself through personal reflection, a strong sense of what you value, and a clear picture of your ideal destination.

Sometimes feedback is simply a wake-up call. What you see in yourself, for whatever reason, is not obvious to others. What you think is working well is not working for someone else! That doesn't mean you are bad or wrong or incompetent. It is what it is—a difference in perception.

Ultimately you get to decide what action is required. Before discounting feedback, process it in a healthy and productive way. Take from it what you can, and put it to work. Make it profitable. And while you seek feedback from others, look inside too. Look inside at the *whole* you.

Like most of the concepts in this book, feedback is not reserved for the *professional* you. Bring feedback home. For several years now I have practiced a reflective thinking exercise taught by John Maxwell in his book *Thinking for a Change: 11 Ways Highly Successful People Approach Life and Work.*[2]

At the end of each day I spend a few moments reflecting on my home and work life. I ask myself five questions:

1. What did I accomplish, or what am I most proud of?

2. What did I learn?

3. What will I do differently tomorrow?

4. What kind of a mother, wife, daughter, friend, or business partner was I today?

5. What needs to change in order for me to become my ideal self, personally and professionally?

Like Maxwell, I have found that developing a set of questions helps me stay focused and consistent with feedback to myself. At the end of each week, I review my notes and look for patterns and trends. I do the same at the end of each month. Once a year I *retreat* to review the past and plan for the future, holding my results and my progress up to my values and ideals. I measure the gaps again, plan to eliminate those, and celebrate my progress. This personal retreat always leaves me feeling refreshed and centered—ready to begin again.

## THE FEEDBACK IS NOT YOU, BUT IT IS YOURS

When you implement these feedback strategies, you will encourage a new direction of growth, invite people to see you in a new light, and highlight your best features. You can even guide others to notice your efforts and your hidden potential. With self-reflection as an important dimension of your feedback, you will remain centered and focused, steadily moving in the direction of your goals and ideals.

The most exciting thing about feedback is that you own it. Feedback does not own you! Do not wait for others to give you what you need to grow. It is yours, so ask for it and make it profitable.

## ATTRACT YOUR NEXT OPPORTUNITY

Training growth is not just about cutting things away. As we've seen with the personal balance sheet, it is also adding to or grafting in. In a garden, specific plants are used to attract what is beautiful and repel what is not. We can draw butterflies, hummingbirds, or even bats! We can do the same thing in our lives. We can attract (or repel) opportunity.

We attract what we make ourselves available for and what we invest ourselves in. That can work for or against us. Much like a self-fulfilling prophecy, we attract what we think about, talk about, and pay attention to. (I've known people who made themselves far too available for gossip, parking lot meetings, or whine fests.) On the other hand, we can strategically attract more opportunity by focusing on steps like these:

1. *Ask for opportunity.* That is to be taken quite literally. Pray for opportunity. Ask your boss for an exciting project. Sign up. Volunteer. Raise your hand and boldly say, "Pick me!"

2. *Fully expect opportunity to arrive.* Every day before your feet hit the floor, remind yourself that opportunity is on the way. You may not see it yet, but it will turn the corner soon. When you fully expect opportunity to arrive, you are less likely to miss it when it does.

3. *Actively search for it!* Opportunity is all around us. Perhaps we don't recognize it because it often comes disguised as problems, questions, trends in the industry, or the latest news.

4. *Create it!* Bring a compelling idea to the table. Don't wait for an assignment; produce a solution! Find a way to make something better.

5. *Negotiate for it.* You may have heard me say it before, and it bears repeating: *absolutely everything is negotiable.* Negotiate for a plum assignment, a more visible role, a new skill, a broader scope of work, or the chance to learn more about other areas of the organization.

6. *Market your personal and professional development.* Communicate your goals, and make your results more visible. Ask for the opportunity to practice an emerging strength or address an area needing development. This is a wonderful way to make your growth obvious.

7. *Build your brand (your reputation) around the opportunities you seek.* Marketers know that there is tremendous power in a brand. To be effective, the brand must be a consistent message, built over time. For example, if you want to be known as *strategic*, look for opportunities to showcase those attributes.

8. *Become a greater resource to your network.* Proactively look for ways to help others succeed. This not only adds value to others, but it also makes you indispensable!

Strategies like these make us top-of-mind when opportunities become available. As one mentor recently asked his mentee, "Why are you not the first person mentioned when a new opportunity is discussed?" What a compelling question! (And here's the just-as-thought-provoking follow-up question, "What do you need to do now to become the first person mentioned next time?")

This can be a difficult proposition depending on your situation. Chris describes her reality this way: "My manager is extremely *low conflict* and *low-key*. Honestly, she works very hard to stay under the radar, and she is succeeding. That makes her virtually invisible within the organization, and that means our team is invisible too. I feel invisible! I don't get a lot of feedback because my manager doesn't have those tools, so sometimes I feel like I am working in a vacuum. She does not proactively market the results of the group. My challenge was to hit the radar without undermining my boss or overstepping the boundaries."

Chris filled the gap with a great mentor and focused on building a sound network throughout the organization. "I found ways to market my results and make my boss and team look good in the same breath. My mentor helped me craft the messages, observe protocols, and discern the fine lines of the organization. Having a mentor with that kind of organizational savvy was critical."

## GRAFTING: HOW DOES YOUR NETWORK GROW?

Randy Lee, a senior vice president for a global technology company, is known throughout his organization as a dynamic mentor and the absolute *master of networking*. At a mentoring conference, I asked him to share how he has built such a viable network.

Here is the advice he offered:

> I seek opportunities to network, and I build networking into everything. Today, for example, in this conference many people will sit with and socialize with people they know and work with. That is their comfort zone, but in doing that they will miss the opportunity to meet new people and broaden their perspective and their network. Tonight, many of us

who have traveled to be here will go back to hotel rooms, order room service, and answer e-mails. If we are serious about networking, we will spend at least part of that time getting to know our colleagues, learning more about what they are trying to accomplish, and building our community.

Other people describe Randy's networking this way: "Randy seeks people out. He asks lots of questions and searches to understand what people are working on and what is getting in the way. He grafts people into his network by connecting people, and in doing all of that, he impacts the business in ways he may not even know."

I encourage you to make networking an absolute priority. Here are six things to consider as you build your strategy:

1. *Build a knowledge base, not a database.* Seek to understand the goals and aspirations of the people in your network. When you understand those pieces, you have positioned yourself as a resource, not a *contact*. (Incidentally, resources are more highly prized than contacts.)

2. *Touch your network frequently.* Set an appointment with yourself each week, even for twenty minutes, to pick up the phone, jot a personal note, or make an introduction.

3. *Build it before you need it.* Recently I encouraged a woman who is looking for a new job to tap into her network. She said (and I quote), "I don't have any friends." We both laughed for a moment at how crazy that sounded, and then she repeated herself, "Really, I don't have any friends." Suddenly it didn't sound so funny—her years of not networking were now a real barrier.

4. *Look at who is on the list and who should be.* Set goals for your network. Whom do you want to add? How can you make that happen? Look at your current network too. How can you help them, and how can they help you?

5. *Build networking in.* Make it your best practice to meet people and make the connections. Meetings, social events, and even waiting in line can be prime opportunities to build your network. Take the social initiative. Throw your hand out, ask questions, and get people talking about their favorite subject…them!

6. *Be on the lookout for information that adds value.* I learned this one from a brilliant networker, Harvey Mackay.[3] If you know the interests and goals of the people in your knowledge base, you can look for information and news relevant to them. Rip out the magazine or newspaper article, jot a quick note, and send it off. I keep stamped envelopes in my briefcase for just this occasion. (I can't tell you how many airline magazines I've ransacked over the years. This works well at the doctor or dentist's office too. *Shhhhh.*)

With these tips in mind, remember that the dynamics of networking have changed. We are wired up and online. E-mail is suddenly the *old-fashioned* way to stay connected and create community. Today we have social utilities like LinkedIn, Plaxo, Facebook, and MySpace. We can post a profile, create connections, stay in touch, recommend a colleague, and publish a virtual résumé online for the world to browse. These tools can serve us, or they can derail us.

As one consultant told the *New York Post,* "Your Google results are your new résumé."[4] There is research suggesting that more and more companies are clicking in to check you out. The lesson here is to leverage networking tools and use them wisely. There are many people (and the number is growing rapidly) who have learned this lesson the hard way—by missing an opportunity they wanted very much because something ridiculous and unprofessional was posted online for the world to see.

Here's a special public service announcement for the young and hip:

---

*Public Service Announcement:*
*You are not immortal, and your past is relevant to your future. Think very carefully about what you hold up for the world to see online. What seems amusing and edgy today will (I absolutely guarantee it) look foolish and immature later. And worse, it may cost you the opportunity you seek. Sometimes first impressions really are last impressions. Clean up your online act!*

---

Managing your feedback, building your network, and attracting opportunity are all pieces of cutting away and grafting in. These are ongoing processes of reflection, course correction, and self-management. Make them conscious, thoughtful strategies to train and promote your growth. If you will do that, you will find yourself growing purposefully in new directions. You will increase your value, and you will create opportunity.

## JOURNALING EXERCISE

1. What do you see in yourself that you wish others would recognize? How can you reveal that strength or ability?

2. What do others see in you that you do not see in yourself? What keeps you from accepting (or appreciating) that part of yourself?

3. What questions will you ask yourself to encourage more self-reflection?

4. What are you doing to attract (or repel) opportunity?

5. How does your network grow?

# 19

# LEARN FROM MASTER GARDENERS

*Find a mentor*

W HEN I WAS A young girl growing up in a small town in Eastern Oregon, my grandfather was my best friend. He was a tall, strong Irishman, and we called him *Pop*. Blinded in a mining accident when he was young, his pursuits still amaze me. He was a farmer, a fisherman, and a gardener.

After my grandmother died, Pop came to live with us. I was a child with vision, and he was an adult with authority. What a wonderful combination! We went all around together. Such a sight we must have been as we walked to town to shop for fishing lures and treats. He had memorized the streets by counting the curbs, and I would test him at each corner to see if he knew where we were. He always did, and that made me feel safe. I felt important too.

I didn't know it then, but today, as I teach the principles of mentoring, I recognize that Pop was a master gardener in my life. I learned profound things from him. From watching him move confidently through life, I learned that the greatest stumbling blocks are on the inside, not the outside. I learned that you are never too young or too small to make a big difference and to have *vision* for another. I learned how to balance myself when someone needed to lean on me for support and how to slow down a bit when the path was uneven.

## WHO ARE THE MASTER GARDENERS IN YOUR LIFE?

Much of the work I do involves mentoring, coaching, and talent management—helping organizations attract, develop, and keep the best people. I am passionate about mentoring because I believe it is one of the most important strategies for personal and professional development available to us. Through mentoring we prepare for our next steps (and in doing that, we make the most of the step we're on). Mentoring builds the heart and forges confidence.

The impact of mentoring is undeniable—for the organization and the individual. Organizations committed to mentoring report the ability to manage change more effectively, prepare the next line of leadership, and attract the most qualified candidates. When organizations make the investment in formal mentoring programs, they fully expect to see results like these:

- Increased retention

- Improved job performance

- Higher quality and productivity

- Leaders ready to take the next step

- Broader understanding of the organization

- Stronger sense of community

From the perspective of those mentored, the benefits are also striking. People who have been mentored tend to earn more, and they are promoted faster. Both of these outcomes may be related to the process of mentoring, which focuses on developing a solid career plan and building a strong professional network. Mentoring *plugs* individuals into the organization and makes professional development a personal priority.

Mentees or protégés are generally exposed to a broader organizational perspective. They are made more visible, and they are able to market themselves more effectively. They see how all of the pieces fit together to form the big picture. This allows them to build strong networks, break through functional barriers, and have greater impact.

More than once, mentees have talked about how mentoring experiences have helped them process and bounce back from disappointing outcomes. On a personal level they felt supported, and on a professional level they came away with a solid plan to improve future results.

I love to ask people what they have learned from the mentors in their lives, and I hear the most wonderful (and often profound) stories.

- *Steve*, a technical account manager from the United Kingdom, tells the story of his grandmother who taught him how to iron a shirt. He was completely frustrated with the task and not at all successful. After ironing the sleeves and moving on to the collar, the sleeves would get rumpled and creased again. It was an exercise in futility. Then his grandmother showed him the proper way to do it—where to begin and how to proceed—how one step impacts the next. That lesson serves him to this day. He learned how to break tasks down into efficient and effective steps. You see, his grandmother wasn't just teaching him how to iron a shirt—she was teaching him how to solve a problem, improve a process, and manage a project.

- *Talitha*, a distribution sales representative from the Bay Area, has learned many things from the mentors in her life, and there is a consistent theme woven throughout. She summarizes the lessons with this profound understanding: "I have learned that just because I am afraid of something doesn't mean I shouldn't be doing it." Her mentors have taught her to step out, step up, and take risks. Talitha has honored that advice time and again. She is a dynamic woman with a dynamic career.

- *Jim*, a sales director from California, was discouraged when he wasn't selected for a promotion. A colleague was chosen instead, and he didn't understand why. He genuinely believed he was the right choice and felt slighted by the decision. As he shared this with a mentor, she wrote something on piece of paper and pushed it across the desk to him. The note read, "You are naïve. Promote yourself." That's when Jim learned it is not just about qualifications; it is about proactively networking and marketing yourself. "Leverage networking technologies and tools," he advises. "Make networking a top priority." That lesson has served him well, and now he shares it as a mentor for his organization.

- *Susan* felt like she had reached a dead end in a technical support role. She wasn't learning anything new, and she desperately needed a challenge. Her mentor worked with her to identify key projects within the organization and ways she might add value to those initiatives. With a clear understanding of the impact she could have and what she could learn through the experience, Susan asked her boss for the opportunity to work on one of the project teams. Her boss agreed and was very impressed with the initiative she demonstrated in researching and proposing the special assignment.

- *Carolyn* worked for a hospital but dreamed of owning her own business. She didn't know where to begin. Her mentors helped her develop a vision and write a business plan. They encouraged her dream and bolstered her confidence. "I would not be where I am now without mentors," she confides. "They didn't do the work for me; they listened, offered counsel, and pointed me toward the resources I needed to make it happen. They believed in me (sometimes more than I believed in myself), and they pushed me out of my comfort zone."

Mentors will see things you don't see. They bring a new perspective—a new way of looking at old things. Mentors help you generate options and push you to explore them.

A good mentor is a sounding board, a trusted advisor, and a visionary. The most successful people can point to mentors who have helped them achieve the level of success they currently enjoy.

## So Who Needs a Mentor?

The short answer is *everyone*, and that includes you. Mentoring is especially helpful if you are in transition, managing change, or preparing for a next step. Mentoring can be the lifeline if you are making a tough decision, dealing with complex problems, or not getting the results you need. It can also help if you are stuck in a rut and need a fresh perspective. Here are a few examples of mentoring making a real impact:

- *Linda* did not know if she wanted to stay on a technical track or position herself for a leadership role. She worked with her mentor to develop two possible career paths. They isolated the skill gaps for both options and found a great deal of overlap. This has allowed Linda

to focus on areas of growth that will not limit her
options. Essentially she is running her possible paths
in parallel and getting ready for both.

- *Karen* wanted to move from an administrative support
position into sales. This was not a typical career move
in her company, and it seemed like one of those "you
can't get there from here" situations. Her mentor
assisted in building her professional network, identifying the necessary skills, and drafting an action plan
that made the transition possible.

- *Susan* was a new manager and not entirely prepared
for the challenges of the position. Within the first
six months, turnover went up and productivity went
down. She was managing friends and former co-
workers (some of whom believed they should have
received the promotion). On more than one occasion
team members went over her head to discuss issues
with her boss. She searched for a mentor who could
help her recover her confidence, build credibility with
her team, and develop her leadership skills. These
strategies not only stabilized her in her current role,
but they also positioned her for higher levels of leadership in the future.

These scenes remind us that mentoring is real-time and custom-
ized. It is not about *doing lunch*. It is development in action where
goals and obstacles are transformed into mentoring moments and
case studies. Outcomes and results in mentoring are important, but
the process is where the real value is. It is what we learn along the
way that puts real topspin on the ball.

One of the best coaching and mentoring lessons I've ever learned was from Hall of Fame baseball pitcher Goose Gossage. Goose was my son's coach for several years in Colorado. For a boy with a baseball dream, he was the ultimate mentor!

There were times when Tabor's game was off. He just didn't have his best *stuff* with him. The ball wasn't doing what he asked of it. These were agonizing innings for Mom! (Have you experienced this? I don't care what the performance is—a recital, a sporting event, or a school play, when your child is on stage and struggling, it is nothing short of excruciating!)

In these moments I would pray, "Take him out. It's not my boy's day! Just take him out." And sometimes Goose would. After just a few pitches, he would call him in. On other occasions, he would let it go on and on. He would leave my son on that mound and me in my seat, sweating it out.

I wondered about the difference between these times, why sometimes he ended it quickly and other times he let it go the distance, so I asked him. And this is what he said: "I will never pull your son from a battle he believes he can win, and I'll never leave him in a battle he believes he can't. I look in his eyes and try to see his heart. It's not a perfect science, and sometimes I may get it wrong, but I make the decision by understanding which *time* he's in."

That's mentoring. It is having the wisdom to know *which time you're in.*

The best mentoring also facilitates self-discovery. It is not about your lending judgment (like a library book that must be returned); it is about creating judgment. Instead of giving the answers, we help others find their own. Rather than tell, we ask questions like these:

- What would you like to try?

- What other options are available?

- How are you getting in your own way?

- What needs to change?

If you don't have a mentor, make this the year to find one! Mentoring is by far one of the most powerful things you can do for your career (and your sanity). We are designed for success, but we are not designed to go it alone! Our lives should come with this disclaimer: *Do not attempt any of this alone!*

## Choosing a Mentor

People often ask how to choose a mentor. Who in your personal or professional life meets these criteria? These guidelines will help you in your choice: Great mentors...

- Believe in personal growth. They are growing and learning. Development is a core value.

- Possess excellent communication skills.

- Are trustworthy.

- Have achieved a level of success or accomplishment you aspire to.

- Can help you make important discoveries and find your blind spots.

- Rather than lending you their judgment, assist you in developing your own.

- Are willing to invest in the success of others.

- Have excellent reputations, marked by integrity.

- Are authentic.

- Are willing to share what they have learned from success and failure.

I encourage you to *test drive* your mentor choices. Run a challenge you are currently facing by them. Ask their opinion about an opportunity. There is so much you can learn from good mentors. For example:

- What has been their greatest career lesson or most notable achievement?

- What skills did they consciously work to develop and master?

- What challenges have they faced, and how did they overcome those?

- What do they value, and how do they reflect and honor those values in their work?

- What steps did they take to get where they are?

In consulting with mentoring communities, I am learning that a holistic approach—one that incorporates life and work goals—is most effective. This kind of mentoring impacts the quality of life, not just the quality (and quantity) of work. It helps us strike a balance between work and life and build the confidence we need to take strategic risks. It challenges us to search our souls for what really matters and helps us put all of it into a healthier perspective.

As you look for a mentor, remember to be one. As you reach forward with one hand, reach back with another and bring someone along. You may have the answer someone else is looking for. Invest yourself in others. It is such a pleasure to watch another person *become.*[1]

## JOURNALING EXERCISE

1. What have been your experiences with mentoring? Think about family members, teachers, coaches, and leaders in your life. What have you learned from them? What are the themes of your mentoring lessons?

2. Choose a difficult scenario—a big decision or an exciting opportunity you are presently facing. Write a detailed description of the situation, and make a list of the people who may be able to give you perspective. At the same time, think about people you admire and respect. How might they see your situation? How would they approach it?

3. Think about your grand design and goals. How could mentors help you move closer to your destiny?

## 20

# GROWING THROUGH ADVERSITY

*Watch for hope to spring forth during
the winter of adversity*

AT THE BEGINNING OF this book I asked if hope is an action or a discipline. Is it faith or science? As these chapters unfold, perhaps you are drawing the same conclusion as I have. Hope is all of these. It comes in many containers, and some of them are most beautiful because they have been broken. I think hope can also be a person. It can be you.

*In times of adversity, people look for leadership, and they look for hope. You can show them both.*

There was once a passenger ship caught in a deadly storm. As the ship was tossed and thrown about on the tempest, many onboard believed all hope was lost. Their fate was sealed; they would perish at sea.

In a last desperate act, one of the passengers fought his way through the gale, finally reaching the wheelhouse to see for himself what was happening. The wind was raging, and the ship was rolling wildly. There he saw the captain who had tied himself to the wheel, fighting the storm with every ounce of his strength to maneuver the ship against this terrible force. The passenger's heart sank. Surely they would not survive.

Then the captain turned to him and smiled. Relieved, the passenger rushed back to tell the others the good news. "Everything will be all right! I saw the captain with my own eyes, and he smiled!"[1]

We may have to secure ourselves to the wheel of life and fight with every ounce of our strength through a storm of adversity. Our ship may toss and roll. We are wise to remember that how we face the storm also gives other people cues and clues. In the storm, we can inspire fear or confidence. Our response to adversity can produce hope. I know this is true. I have seen the captain smile.

When Tish was diagnosed with a rare and deadly cancer—when fear would have liked to grip us all, I saw the captain smile. In this storm, the captain was her father, John Hagee, a mighty man of faith. He responded to his daughter's diagnosis like a warrior called to battle, and Tish met the challenge with amazing faith, grace, and courage.

She shared journal entries along the way, and they were remarkable—a wonderful mix of authenticity, faith, and humor. As I read these, I thought of the people who would be inspired by her experience and draw strength from it. Tish's story is nothing short of miraculous. She is more than a survivor. Her experience produced strength, and it is still producing hope.

In the late eighties and early nineties, the banking industry was extremely volatile. Again, I saw the captain smile. His name was Eric, and at that time he was senior partner of the largest savings bank in the Pacific Northwest. He was also my boss and a wonderful mentor. When the institution we worked for was purchased by another institution, he smiled and said, "We still have some time left. Let's do something remarkable with it."

Those last months were not fear filled. They were exciting and full of purpose. When it was finally time to go, we were ready for the next adventure, full of confidence and proud of what we had accomplished. His leadership inspired confidence and loyalty. What could have been a time of holding on to the rails for dear life became a season of greatness—the last inning of a game well played. I can still hear Eric saying, "We've hit the ball right out of the park!"

When Stephanie lost her husband, she was paralyzed with grief for months. "I was absolutely numb," she shared with me over dinner. "There are months that I don't even remember. I dreaded going home after work. To be alone in the home I had shared with the love of my life and my best friend was just too painful."

Now you will find Stephanie leading a support group for people who are grieving. As she told me her story, I was moved by all that she has been through and with how she has turned her painful experiences into hope for others. She has recycled the pain, and she is exporting hope. As I speak with her now, she is absolutely passionate about this mission of support. "I want to do more. I know I can do more."

Stephanie's journey has not been an easy one, but there has been such purpose in the pain. Her experiences have created an incredible capacity to understand what others are going through—where they are in the process of grief and what they need to move forward and heal. As she looks back on the story of her life, she sees how each step prepared her for the one she is on now. When Stephanie works with people in the throes of grief, they see the captain smile.

I believe that very special people are sometimes trusted with very difficult things. God allows them to face challenges that are very difficult to bear because He can trust them and empower them in those circumstances. He knows they will turn tragedy and challenge into victory. They will grow through the pain, and they will transform it into something extraordinary.

*Sometimes faith must firmly grasp the hand of hope to steady her knees and give her strength.*

Every life will eventually face a storm. Our adversity may be the loss of someone we love or a serious illness. Or it may come in the failure of a relationship, the loss of a job, or the death of a dream. We have not been promised a *cakewalk* through life. We have been promised that we do not walk alone.

> The LORD will guide you always;
>   he will satisfy your needs in a sun-scorched land
>   and will strengthen your frame.
> You will be like a well-watered garden,
>   like a spring whose waters never fail.
> —ISAIAH 58:11, NIV

If you have dared to dream a big dream and things have not worked the way you planned, don't be tempted to give up or give in. It may seem easier to revert to an old story when the new one is harder to write than you believed. It is instinctual to return to what we understand, even if what we understand is unhealthy, unchallenging, and unrewarding. But the struggle to reach your dream will be well worth the effort.

Years ago I came across a beautiful story originally told by Earl Nightingale.[2] A small boy in India was walking down a dirt road. In the distance he spied an old man sitting under a tree. As the boy drew closer, he saw the old man was holding something carefully in his hands. Overcome by curiosity, the child asked, "What do you have?"

Slowly, the old man opened his hands to reveal a cocoon. The child didn't understand the science of metamorphosis—caterpillars transforming into butterflies, so the old man patiently explained it to him. This completely intrigued the boy, and he asked the elder if he might hold it. His wish was granted.

Emboldened, he asked, "Can I have it? I want to take it home so I can see the butterfly when it escapes the cocoon!"

The old man considered this request for a moment and finally agreed, but with one important condition. He told the child, "When the cocoon opens and you see the butterfly, you must not touch it. You must promise to open the window and set it free."

Barely able to contain his excitement, the child promised.

The boy gently carried the butterfly home and placed it on the windowsill. Day after day he watched. Just when he imagined nothing would ever happen, he noticed the cocoon was cracking open! When he came very close, with an eye almost touching it, he thought he could see the brilliant blue and gold wings.

Terribly excited, he threw open the window and pulled up a chair to watch his butterfly take flight. But it didn't. It was turning and twisting inside of the cocoon. For the longest time (what seemed like an eternity for the child), the butterfly battled against the walls of this prison. The child realized his butterfly was hopelessly trapped!

He waited until he couldn't stand it for another second. Unsure of how to help (after all, whom do you ask about stuck butterflies), he pulled the cocoon open with clumsy fingers. The butterfly flopped out and became completely still.

The boy knew his butterfly would never fly. Clutching it tightly, he ran in search of the old man. He found his elder sitting beneath the same tree, almost looking as if he expected to see this heartbroken child with a dead butterfly in his small fist. The child cried out, "My butterfly did not fly!"

The old man replied, "You touched it, didn't you?"

Admitting that he did, the boy explained that the butterfly had been hopelessly trapped and needed his help.

The old man understood. "What you didn't know was that the turning and twisting inside the cocoon was forcing blood into the tissue-like wings of the butterfly. When you took away the struggle, you took away all possibility of flight."

When I tell that story now, it resonates with people. I can see and feel people connecting with it, understanding it on a very personal level. Maybe this story simply speaks straight to the heart, saying, "I understand you. I know about your struggle, and it is not without purpose."

---

## *Public Service Announcement: You are not stuck.*

---

Our storms will test us, and our goals will stretch us. (That's what goals are for. If they don't stretch us, they aren't called goals. They are called *to dos*.) I am learning that God doesn't *touch the butterfly*. He allows the struggle because He longs to see the flight.

When adversity knocks on the door of your life, these are the techniques that help you to stay the course and make the turn:

- Acknowledge what you are going through and what you are feeling.

- Take extra care of yourself, for adversity requires strength.

- Reach out for support and surround yourself with Calebs.

- Review your notes on change! Focus on the pieces you can impact, and leave the rest to God. (I promise He knows the end of the story, and He isn't up there somewhere wringing His hands. He is throwing open a window and waiting for you to take flight!)

Adversity may be like winter in the garden—barren and cold, with shortened days and longer nights. Remember that winter is a season, and spring comes next! When spring comes, you will be like the tree that survived winter and said, "I have survived the winter, and I have grown!"[3]

When you look back upon the struggles of life, I hope you will find a place for gratitude. It is the struggle that forced blood through your *wings* so you could fly. If you are experiencing adversity and great resistance now, you may actually be running the best race of your life against the wind. The stopwatch may not reflect it, but you are developing incredible strength and resiliency. You may not feel or see that just now, but you will in the days to come. Look for your captains, and you will see them smile.

### Journaling Exercise

1. Who are the captains in your life, and how have they inspired confidence in the storm?

2. How has adversity produced hope in your life?

3. In what ways have you recycled pain to export hope?

4. If you are in a storm, what pieces of the situation do you control?

# 21

# PULLING COMPLACENCY

*Complacency is the decision to take
the path of least resistance*

THERE IS A HOUSE in my town that made me very sad. For years it had been neglected and run down. Once beautiful, it had become an object of much tongue-clucking criticism.

You know the house. You probably have one like it in your town too. It's the one you drive by and say, "What a shame," and "Why do people let their yard go to seed like that?" It's the house where the neighbors have given up complaining and resigned themselves to plant taller hedges and build higher fences to block the depressing view.

Then something wonderful happened! A hard-working couple with a grand vision bought this neglected beauty. Almost overnight, the transformation began. They worked tirelessly inside and out. They cleared and pulled, planted and groomed the landscape. I loved driving by to see the amazing progress. The house quickly became the jewel of the neighborhood. The tongue clucking ceased; you could almost hear a collective sigh of relief.

When we learned the couple was relocating, we were so disappointed. In its newly improved condition, the house sold quickly, and a nice new family moved in. Now the wonderful landscape is slipping away. The hedges are losing their shape; vines are growing up through them now, choking them back. The lush lawn is plagued with weeds and creeping bare spots.

When I drive by the house, I wonder, "Did the new owners believe their landscape would remain pristine with no effort or maintenance, or are they just too busy? Do they even see how quickly their investment is declining? Do they understand that what attracted them to this home in the first place is at risk?"

This house teaches me that gardens need care and attention. *Neglect equals decline.* It reminds me to ask myself, "What (or who) are you taking for granted right now? What is at risk in your own garden?"

I often use an uncomfortable exercise in values to make this point. If you are up to it, I invite you to try it now. Write down (in the journal I trust you are keeping faithfully) three things you value most. These must be in priority order—listed as one, two, and three. There can only be one number 1, and so on. (If you have three children, I am not suggesting that you choose between them. You can make *children or family* one of your priorities.)

Once you have the three values listed, focus on the third item. As painful as it may be, I want you to imagine your life without this. If this treasure was gone forever from your life and you could never retrieve it, what would your life be like? (If you are doing this correctly, your throat is probably getting tight, and a knot is forming in your stomach.)

Move on to the second item on your list. Again, if this were taken from you, what would your life be like? (The knot in your stomach is probably moving to your throat. I've even seen people weep at the very thought of losing what is so precious.) You are not quite finished. Look at the first item on your list. I've had people literally shout out in a conference, "I won't give you number one! You cannot have my number one!"

Why? It's because life without this would be too painful, too lonely, or too hopeless.

Honestly, this is a very emotional exercise. It is horrible to think of the things we treasure disappearing from our lives. The good news is that you can have (and keep) what you value *if* you take care of it and focus on it. Hold on to these values tightly. Let your time, your goals, and your priorities reflect what you treasure the most. Ensure that your boundaries protect them—complacency is never allowed to grow here!

We take for granted the things that are working—or appear to be. These are the things or people not screaming for our attention in this whirlwind we call life. And thank goodness for that, because if one more thing demanded your attention, you might just come unglued.

Managers take for granted the high-performing employee who works consistently and independently. This is the employee you can count on... for anything and everything. (And you do.) This is the first person you think of when you need something done, because when you give her a project, you are certain it will be taken care of. This isn't intentional indifference. The days are jam-packed with problems and issues and employees who can't or *won't* work like that.

We take our health for granted—until it fails. I'll always remember the wise words of Dr. Don Colbert, who recommended a wellness program for my husband and me. The plan included significant changes (a complete overhaul, actually) in our diet, exercise, and nutritional supplements. As he reviewed the action plan with us, he said, "Remember, you catch a cold—you don't catch a disease. Diseases are developed over time by the choices you make. Health is cheap. Disease is expensive." (Incidentally, our visit to Dr. Colbert was inspired by a health scare—otherwise known as a physical wake-up call.)

We may even take for granted our skill set and knowledge. After all, we've been doing this job for years. We've forgotten more about this job than most people will ever learn! If we don't continue learning and growing, looking for ways to improve, we are becoming obsolete.

A young, dynamic professional tells this story of her heart-breaking encounter with complacency.

Kim was a few years out of college, just married, and beginning an aggressive climb up the corporate ladder. Her career was really taking off. Both her job and her husband's were extremely demanding; they actually thrived on the fast pace, long hours, impossible deadlines, and relentless travel.

Throughout the day they communicated with text messages, e-mail, and voice mail. At least each night there was a goodnight kiss, even if it was long distance by cell phone. They kiddingly referred to this late night call as "syncing up."

Kim was grateful her husband understood the nontraditional hours. He understood the project that caused her to miss dinner, his birthday, and their second anniversary. He understood completely, because he missed them too. Their lives could best be described as two highways running in perfect parallel.

She wept the day she realized they were no longer running in parallel. How did that happen? When did that happen? Somewhere along the way, the roads had turned. They did not intersect. The late-night calls became voice mails, and even when they found themselves in the same room, they couldn't find anything meaningful to say. They were more like roommates working different shifts and crossing paths occasionally.

With dozens of professional commendations, a giant title, and an even bigger paycheck, Kim is now working on the most important project of all—her marriage. I wish her well, and I pray she and her husband find that intersection. I thank her for her story, because it reminds me that when we take for granted what is working, we may find out down the road it isn't working anymore.

Complacency creates a vacuum; what fills that vacuum is dangerous. It puts us at great risk. Use these questions to test your life for complacency:

1. What are you taking for granted?

2. What is running on *autopilot* in your life?

3. What values are reflected in your calendar and your schedule?

4. How do your commitments reflect and protect what you value the most?

5. What needs to change?

Complacency requires a compromise. I invite you to test that theory. Whenever I evaluate complacency, I find a compromise of value or integrity. Even the home in my town with the overgrown yard reflects a compromise. Something was determined to be more important or valued more highly than taking care of the lawn and garden.

This may be entirely fair. There may be something going on in that home far more important than grass and trees. The point is still the same. Complacency requires a compromise. We make choices, and something *gives*.

But more often than not, I find complacency is not the result of something more important that is going on in *the house*. In my experience, complacency is often the conscious or unconscious decision to take the easier route—the path of least resistance.

When a manager neglects and overburdens a star performer, by default she is valuing results over people. She compromises the performer to get those results. (It is easier to get more from a performing employee and harder to confront nonperformance.) By taking that route, she actually punishes her top performer and indirectly rewards nonperformance. She is not doing the effective thing. She is doing the expeditious thing.

Small compromises in what we eat or how we treat our bodies can add up to major health concerns. It is easier and faster to whip through the drive-through, talk to the box, and get dinner in a bag.

We compromise our personal development when we don't make the investment in ourselves to keep learning and improving our skills. It is very hard to pull away from the demands of the job and make time for training. Honestly, I am amazed at the number of employees who don't take advantage of the training opportunities available within their organizations. Time and again, the same people show up (and the same people don't). It is actually a bit amusing. The people who may need training the most aren't there (unless compelled by the word *mandatory*). When I speak on anger management, for example, the angry people usually don't come. It's those trying to cope with the angry people who show up!

Sometimes arrogance opens the door for complacency. When we think we have all the answers, we stop asking questions, and if we don't see a problem, we won't ask for or receive help. The very definition of *complacency* is a wake-up call: "self-satisfaction, especially when accompanied by unawareness of actual dangers or deficiencies."

I was once asked to consult an organization on a serious ethical issue concerning a senior officer. As we discussed what the organization must do to repair and restore the situation, my client shook her head in disbelief and asked, "How did we get here?" This answer was easy. For the organization, it was a lack of awareness about a real danger. They fell asleep at the wheel, and the ship ran aground.

In all of these scenarios, can you see how choices move people closer to (or further from) the real intention? *Living with intention requires that we pay close attention to the choices we make and where those choices take us.* Where you are standing now in every area of your life is a direct reflection of the choices you have made—by design or by default. In this context, a nonaction is an action. No decision really is a decision.

All of this really is wonderful news! If you don't like where you are, you can begin this moment to make different choices. Here's a little push out of complacency:

1. *Invest in your future.* One of my *virtual* mentors, author Brian Tracy, offers this advice: "Invest three percent of your income in yourself (self-development) in order to guarantee your future."[1] This counsel has served me very well.

2. *Take a risk!* Sometimes the fear of failure keeps us from stepping out. What looks like apathy and indifference is really a lack of confidence. Give yourself permission to try and to fail! (And while you're at it, give yourself more chances at success.)

3. *Raise the standard.* Have you settled into a level of performance that is less than your best? Recommit to delivering your best effort in everything you do.

4. *Increase your curiosity.* Become genuinely interested in making things better. This includes relationships, processes, skills, and results. Complacency cannot live where continuous improvement is a discipline.

5. *Develop more discipline.* Most of us *know* more than we *do*. Discipline is putting what we know into practice (even when we don't feel like it).

Pulling up complacency protects the work you have done up to this point. Gardens, even beautiful ones, need attention. In fact, the most beautiful gardens are the most cared-for gardens. You've done the hard work of clearing and the thoughtful work of planting. Protect all of that by weeding out complacency and compromise.

## JOURNALING EXERCISE

1. Do a beliefs check. How is complacency reflected in what you believe about yourself and your possibility?

2. What are you frustrated about but unwilling to change?

3. What are you accepting that you could be making better?

4. Review your balance wheel for the areas of your life that are working well. These are your strongest scores. What can you do to keep complacency from creeping in?

## 22

# KEEP ALL OF YOUR APPOINTMENTS WITH HOPE

*Reinforce hope and positive expectancy in your
own life by planting it in the life of another*

A S I WRITE ABOUT hope, a wonderful, hardworking man
named Antonio is recovering from cancer surgery. Antonio
helps us take care of our flowers; he is a much-loved
gardener in my life. He is a wonderful father and husband, grandfather, talented landscaper, and my friend.

With pressing deadlines and project plans for this book, this
morning I sat down to work. Then it dawned on me. Today is not a
day for speaking and writing about hope. Today is a day for doing.
Hope is also an action—hope has legs. I put away my work and went
to visit Antonio in the hospital, and I will always remember this
appointment with hope.

He looked so vulnerable and quiet lying there, not at all as I
pictured him. I remembered him smiling and laughing with his
sons as they worked. I remembered bringing him strong coffee as he
scolded me about, *"Los perros gordos...* something, something... *en
las flores."* (Apparently this is some problem about fat basset hounds
stepping on flowers.) We laughed at his English and my Spanish, but
somehow we managed to get the messages through.

Today I came prepared with a blessing in Spanish. A friend helped
me write it, and as I pulled out one of my famous index cards and
stumbled along—trying so hard to say the words just right—my voice
cracked, my hands trembled, and my eyes filled up and then spilled
over. I wanted so badly to say it right.

He smiled then, and a tear ran down his cheek too. Patiently he waited for me to finish the blessing. Then he reached up, put his hand on my forehead, and spoke the blessing back to me perfectly. I was glad I had come. Hope is the gift that lifts two hearts—yours and another's. The one who carries the blessing becomes the one who is blessed.

I don't want to miss any appointments with hope. I want to be tuned in, ready to go, and available. And even if I can't get the words exactly right, I believe the message of hope will find a way through.

> He will be like a tree planted by the water
>> that sends out its roots by the stream.
> It does not fear when heat comes;
>> its leaves are always green.
> It has no worries in a year of drought
>> and never fails to bear fruit.
>
> —JEREMIAH 17:8, NIV

## THE GROUND COVER OF ENCOURAGEMENT

My first spring experience in Texas was like unwrapping a beautiful gift. As if on cue, wildflowers appeared everywhere! Blankets of them painted the hill country and roadsides. Driving from Austin to Houston, I literally could not believe my eyes. It was spectacular. Later I learned this was the work of Lady Bird Johnson. In 2007, Lady Bird passed on, but her legacy lives in millions of blooms—in the seeds she cast to make this a more beautiful place.

*Each of us has the power to plant the seeds of hope, to help others persevere and accomplish great things—to inspire greatness in another life. What a legacy we can leave!*

You can encourage others to push through obstacles, find new approaches, or explore new options. You have already discovered one way to plant encouragement into the life of another. It is with the words we speak to them, about them, and over them. It is giving others a vision of what is possible. In this chapter, you will identify more ways to infuse people with hope through encouragement.

You can put these concepts to use immediately by thinking of specific people as you read. Who in your life or work:

- ...has suffered a disappointment or a setback?

- ...has overcome an obstacle or achieved a goal?

- ...is facing a significant challenge?

- ...is at the threshold of a marvelous opportunity?

- ...is struggling with an important decision?

- ...is discouraged?

All of these people are candidates for encouragement! Here are a dozen ways you can be the one to deliver the message of hope. This list is for husbands and wives, parents, grandparents, friends, colleagues, and leaders. Everything here is within your power to do and will leave everyone in your life better than you found them.

1. *Be available and present.* Listen, ask questions, and show genuine interest in others. Listening is a skill, and many of us aren't very good at it. There is so much in us that we want to *tell*. If the truth be told, maybe we are better at pretending to listen or just waiting for our turn to talk.

2. *Go out of your way to acknowledge and validate others.* Make this an absolute priority. You may never fully know the difference you have made by simply noticing the effort or achievement of another. For you, the encounter may seem insignificant, even forgettable.

215

For the other, it could be the difference between giving up and pressing on.

3. *Get people involved.* Ask for their opinions, and whenever you can, act on their ideas. Engage and include people in the challenges and the opportunities. Make them a part of the process and the solution.

4. *Highlight progress.* Make a big deal out of even small steps. You may never know how much effort or courage the small step required.

5. *Show genuine appreciation for people*—not just for what they *do*, but also for who they intrinsically *are*. Talk about what you value in them and what you admire about them.

6. *Help see a dream through.* You are that powerful! You have the power to help usher in another's dream.

7. *Encourage risk taking.* Sometimes you rob people of growth when you do too much for them. You become a crutch, and people do not run well on crutches. (Sometimes we get a little ego-fix out of the deal. It feels good to have someone look to us and lean on us. We need to get over that and give people the chance to find out they really can stand on their own.)

8. *Help others see the progress or even the purpose inside of their struggle.* When we are in the middle of the storm, we may not see how much we are growing.

9. *Remind people of the promise.* Help them see the possibilities and build a strong vision of the future. Lend them your faith if they are running low.

10. *Celebrate achievements in meaningful ways.* Success inspires success.

11. *Remind people who they are and what they are capable of.* An organization had gone through a particularly difficult time. I was asked to motivate and build the team. After spending just a few moments with this group, I realized they didn't need to be motivated. They needed to remember who they were. In the wake of change, facing a mountain of challenge, they had forgotten who they were and what they were capable of. We spent the rest of that morning working through a process called *Appreciative Inquiry.* That is simply reflecting on past successes and how they had created those victories. After just a few hours of reflecting on success, the team left standing taller, feeling refreshed, and very clear on their ability to win again.

12. *Reveal options.* When we feel stuck in our situation, we don't see options—we see obstacles. Encourage others and give them a sense of personal control by helping them locate viable options.

These are some of the ways we *cast the seeds* and invest ourselves in others. Often we cast seeds by what we can share with another. Sometimes we cast seeds by simply listening—by being present and working to understand what another may be going through. As Plato said, "Be kind, for everyone you meet is fighting a hard battle." In the everyday living of life, we have countless opportunities to lift the head and lighten the load of people who are in the middle of hard battles.

Empathy is one of the most powerful gifts that we can give another human being. Empathy is different from sympathy. Sympathy agrees with you. Empathy simply tries to understand. I learned about empathy from a gate agent at the Dallas/Fort Worth airport.

I was on my way to Boston, and it was a bad travel day. There was weather everywhere, and hundreds of flights were being canceled, including mine. I positioned myself in the customer service line, which, incidentally, was wrapping itself around the terminal and growing longer by the minute.

This irritated me. I think the term *customer service line* is an oxymoron. (There should be no line in customer service—ever.) Even so, I was twenty-fifth in a line that looked over a hundred. The people were frustrated and growing hostile, and the young woman at the counter was doing a marvelous job of provoking everyone. (She was horrible, really.)

I believe that in every communication you should go in knowing exactly what you want out of it. Have an objective. As I watched this rude young gate agent, my objective became crystal clear. My objective was to make this rude, rude woman cry.

With that mission in mind, I began preparing a speech that would put this horrible person in her place. I was thinking that all of the people in front of me should move aside, because I was actually doing a public service. I would take care of this woman for everyone.

My speech was coming along nicely, when the *good* Dondi popped out on my shoulder and reminded me, "Walk your talk. Be kind. Leave her better than you found her." I silenced that voice immediately. I was a woman with a message, and I was going to deliver it!

As I stepped up to the counter, this thought suddenly occurred to me: my real objective *was not* to make this woman cry; my real objective was to get to Boston. (And I had used all my extra minutes preparing for the wrong objective.)

Fortunately I remembered my tools, and I found something empathetic to say: "I cannot even imagine how it must feel to stand behind that counter and have more than a hundred people lined up waiting to yell at me. I would be overwhelmed."

That's when she burst into tears.

Then she taught me something I will never forget. She said, "I don't control when the planes come or go. I do have some control over who sits on them and where. When this happens, I save one seat in first class for the person who is kind. First-class behavior deserves a first-class seat." I learned from this woman that empathy quite literally gets you where you want to go! But that wasn't the most important lesson.

The moment I stopped judging this woman and tried to understand how it might feel to be her, all of my angst disappeared. I no longer saw her as a horrible person who deserved to cry. I saw a service professional working without the tools, skills, authority, or support she needed to be successful. Once I understood, I didn't have to work at being *nice*. Nice came naturally, like breathing.

Don't get me wrong. I still do not agree with her behavior, but I can understand it. I think I did leave her a little better than I found her (and I enjoyed a complimentary first-class seat to Boston).

She taught me a priceless lesson. Even in the day-to-day, routine interactions with people I may never see again, I can make a difference. I can plant seeds in gardens I will never sit in. As John Maxwell writes, "When we help people feel valuable, capable, and motivated, we sometimes see their lives change forever…and then see them go on to change the world."[1]

Hope and positive expectancy are motivators. We can't, after all, be motivated to achieve something we believe is impossible or futile or that we are powerless to achieve. (When hope leaves the building, motivation is packing her desk.) We won't be motivated to do things that have no purpose or meaning for us, because motivation is *the reason for the action; it gives purpose and direction to behavior.*

Organizations and managers often struggle with this illusive thing called *motivation*. It is a common and pressing question: "How can we motivate these people?" Honestly, I don't think motivating people is the real problem. When I dig into the culture to identify what's at the root of low motivation and morale, I often find the organization is unwittingly demotivating employees with miles of red tape, stifling bureaucracy, and ridiculous policies. Time and again, I find the better questions may be:

- What are we doing right now to demotivate our employees?

- What are we doing to discourage them?

- How are we sucking the life out of our people?

When I ask employees (at any level of an organization) to think of a time when they were extremely motivated or unmotivated, and what contributed to feeling that way, these items usually appear on the list.

| Motivators | Demotivators |
|---|---|
| Being trusted with important assignments | Responsibilities that are not challenging |
| The opportunity to demonstrate skill and specialized knowledge | Reaching a dead end with no opportunities for growth |
| Being asked for opinions and ideas | Having no opportunity to influence decisions |
| Feeling heard, respected, and valued | Feeling excluded or shut out |
| Sincere acknowledgment | Lack of acknowledgment or recognition |
| Being self-managed | Being micromanaged |
| Belonging to a high-performing team or work group | Belonging to a team with an obscure or poor reputation |
| Challenging and realistic goals | Goals that are unrealistic |

| Motivators | Demotivators |
|---|---|
| Having ideas championed and implemented | Not receiving credit for ideas or, worse yet, having a superior take the credit |

The motivators on this list could easily be called *seeds of encouragement*. These are the things that inspire performance and bring wind to the sails. The demotivators knock the air right out of people. Both columns can easily be applied to our personal lives—to our families and other groups we interact with.

From a parent's perspective, I can look at these lists and recognize things I've done both to motivate and to frustrate my son. (I wish he had come with a list like this. I would have done some things differently.) As a leader, I think I've done some of these things well, and I know I've missed some great opportunities to engage hearts and inspire people to greatness. It is important to get this right, especially in roles of authority. When we have authority over people, we have a responsibility to them.

Perhaps one of the most powerful things we can do in life is to develop an appetite for winning. No one (I repeat, no one) wakes up in the morning thinking, "I hope I can lose a little more today." We all want to win, but many of us don't expect to. We don't expect to win because we don't know (or we have forgotten) what winning *tastes* like. What would happen if we expected to win more, and what if we could teach others to do the same?

The answer is something very powerful...something terribly exciting: *you create an appetite for winning by tasting and experiencing wins.*

To celebrate my birthday, my husband often treats to me a swim with the beluga whales at SeaWorld. This is an incredible experience. I have learned more about motivation in a wetsuit than in any book I've ever read. Clients have even joined me on this field trip. Without exception, they leave with a deeper understanding of and stronger commitment to drawing the best out of people.

Performance is strictly *voluntary* for the whales. They are never forced to participate. Trainers must rely on the *want to* factors. So what makes a whale *want to*? Probably many of the same things that make people want to. Here is a short list:

1. Trainers study the whales to understand what *floats their boat,* so to speak. One whale loves a certain toy and another wants the trainer to dive in and play. He doesn't want things; he wants time. The point is, different things inspire the whales and bring the best out of them. The trainers work hard to understand what that something is. They pay close attention to the unique personalities and preferences.

2. Positive reinforcement is always used. There is a whole lot of cheering and applause when the whales are successful. The trainers aren't afraid of looking a little goofy to celebrate success.

3. Relationship is an essential element. There is a genuine devotion and enormous trust between the whales and the trainers. There is also a deep respect.

4. Trainers know that what takes months to build can be destroyed very quickly if they are inconsistent or disregard the needs of the whale.

As I review the list, I wonder: What if we treated people like this? I'd love to find out.

When we plant hope and positive expectancy into the life of another, we reinforce those things in our own lives. It is impossible to carry and cast the seeds of hope without some of them spilling out of the sack along the way. Then comes spring, and the seeds cast will brilliantly color the landscape of our lives with blankets of encouragement.

## Journaling Exercise

1. How can you plant more seeds of encouragement into the lives of others?

2. As you review the motivating and demotivating factors, what would you add? What has motivated or demotivated you?

3. How can you do more of what motivates and inspires others at work and at home?

4. How can you help another person achieve his or her own greatness?

5. What appointments with hope are on your calendar now?

## Reflections

## Part III: Seeds of Hope

Through the pages of this book, you have learned to become the master gardener of your own destiny. Each section of the book contained important principles for you to use. You began by clearing the ground—pulling out of your life the *weeds* that were hindering growth. Then you followed the steps of planting the *seeds* of expectancy. In this final section you discovered how to groom the landscape of challenge and adversity, allowing *perennial hope* to burst forth into realized destiny. Remember the following principles for a garden filled with the blooms of fulfilled blessings.

- When tied to a trellis, a vine designed to grow and climb will do both of these things beautifully. The potential for that is in the seed, and you have already learned that whatever seeds are, they become.

- Like old maps and old stories, continually doing what you have always done will bring you back to old places, the places you have been before. Repeat after me: "What got me here will not take me one step further. To have more or become more, I will have to do new things."

- Hope flourishes when you are fully invested in what you love—what you are passionate about—and when you are growing and making a real difference. Hope grows when you build on your natural strengths and talents, honoring your gifts and *growing with the grain*.

- There is no such thing as a dead end for you—not in your career or in any goal you may set for yourself!

- Paths are personal things. Each is unique, just as unique as the person who travels them. So you shouldn't wait for someone to roll out the corporate rug. It is up to you to build your own road.

- For a life trying to grow, feedback is essential; it is one of the tools you use to train your growth. You leverage feedback when you learn to do two things well— know where to find feedback, and how to process it effectively.

- When it comes to feedback, you are wise to remember that people give you what they have, not necessarily what you need.

- You will attract what you make yourself available for and what you invest yourself in. That can work for or against you. Much like a self-fulfilling prophecy, you attract what you think about, talk about, and pay attention to.

- Mentors will see things you don't see. They bring a new perspective—a new way of looking at old things. Mentors help you generate options and push you to explore them. A good mentor is a sounding board, a trusted advisor, and a visionary.

- As you look for a mentor, remember to be one. As you reach forward with one hand, reach back with another and bring someone along. You may have the answer someone else is looking for. Invest yourself in others. It is such a pleasure to watch another person *become*.

- In times of adversity, people look for leadership, and they look for hope. You can show them both.

- You are not stuck.

- Living with intention requires that you pay close attention to the choices you make and where those choices take you.

- You have the power to plant the seeds of hope, to help others persevere and accomplish great things, and to inspire greatness in another life. What a legacy you can leave!

- You create an appetite for winning by tasting and experiencing wins.

- Keep all of your appointments with hope.

My beloved responded and said to me,
"Arise, my darling, my beautiful one,
And come along.
For behold, the winter is past,
The rain is over and gone.
The flowers have already appeared in the land;
The time has arrived for pruning the vines,
And the voice of the turtledove has been heard in our land.
The fig tree has ripened its figs,
And the vines in blossom have given forth their fragrance.
Arise, my darling, my beautiful one,
And come along!"

—SONG OF SOLOMON 2:10–13, NAS

## CONCLUSION

# HOPE PERENNIAL

As I finish this project, it is nearly dawn in San Antonio, Texas. A steady spring rain is falling outside, soaking the flowers Antonio has planted in the garden. My heart is full, because this book has been a labor of love. It seems so fitting that as I write the last pages, spring and sunlight are bursting through.

When we began this journey, I said, "If I could give you one gift, I would choose hope." Now I know it would not be hope *fully grown*. I would give you *seeds of hope*, so that you might cast them and watch them grow.

I pray what you have found here is like a gentle rain falling onto your life, reminding you of spring, refreshing your spirit, and calling forth your hope perennial. I've been speaking a lot for "Hope." If "Hope" personified were to write you a letter, I think she might say:

Dear One,

You were designed for success. On the day you were born, the Creator of all things breathed destiny into you. You are unique and essential. You have a purpose, and you are more powerful then you might imagine.

Clear the ground and pull out what will choke me from your life. Plant me deep in your heart. Plant me in every compartment of your life. Plant me in your work and in your relationships. If you will plant me, I will grow.

Cast the seeds of hope, and watch with great expectancy! The garden of your life will become more beautiful with each season. What begins small—even shoebox size—will flourish with time and attention.

There will be days when you won't feel like doing any of these things. Do them anyway. You will never regret doing the right thing in the right moment. And that is the beauty of hope—what it produces in you and through you is amazing.

Keep all of your appointments with me. What may look small and insignificant to you in the moment may be a pivotal turning point in the life of another—the difference between giving up and going on.

Guard yourself from complacency. Let nothing quietly creep into your life that will crowd me out. Let me be perennial in your life.

HOPE

As you close the pages of this book, I leave you with this blessing.

May the rooms of your life be filled with what you love the most;
May laughter echo through your hallways;
May your roof shelter people who are weary on the way;
May opportunity shine through every window;
And may hope grow wild in your garden.

# NOTES

## CHAPTER 1
## ROOT BOUND

1.    Noelle Nelson, "Beliefs About the Future," *Futurist Magazine,* January 2000.

2.    Brian Tracy, *The Psychology of Achievement,* audiobook (Niles, IL: Nightingale, 2000).

3.    Robert K. Merton, *Social Theory and Social Structure,* Enlarged Ed edition (New York: Free Press, 1968).

4.    Dondi Scumaci, *Designed for Success: Ten Commandments for Women in the Workplace* (Lake Mary, FL: Excel Books, 2008).

## CHAPTER 2
## EXPERIENCE CAN BE A BAD TEACHER

1.    Jim Collins, *Good to Great: Why Some Companies Make the Leap…and Others Don't* (New York: Collins Business, 2001).

## CHAPTER 3
## HELPLESS BECOMES HOPELESS

1.    Stephen R. Covey, *The 7 Habits of Highly Effective People* (New York: Free Press, 1989, 2004), 93.

2.    Martin E. P. Seligman, *Helplessness: On Depression, Development, and Death* (San Francisco: W.H. Freeman & Co., 1975).

3.    Sam Vaknin, *Malignant Self-Love: Narcissism Revisited* (Czech Republic: Narcissus Publications, 2001).

4.    Alison Mueller, "Antidote to Learned Helplessness: Empowering Youth Through Service," *Reclaiming Children and Youth,* volume 14, 2005.

## CHAPTER 4
## REJECTING REJECTION

1.    Don Colbert, MD, *The Bible Cure for Autoimmune Diseases* (Lake Mary, FL: Siloam, 2004).

2.    Covey, *The 7 Habits of Highly Effective People.*

3.    Charles Stanley, "Self-Rejection: Its Characteristics, Causes and Cures," January 1990 radio message.

## CHAPTER 5
## SHALLOW GROUND

1. Dr. Nathaniel Branden, "Self-Esteem FAQ," National Association for Self-Esteem, http://www.self-esteem-nase.org/faq.php (accessed November 11, 2008).

2. Ibid.

3. Jane E. Brody, "Personal Health: Girls and Puberty: the Crisis Years," *New York Times*, http://www.nytimes.com/specials/women/warchive/971104_1097.html (accessed October 13, 2008).

4. Nicole Hawkins, PhD, "Battling Our Bodies? Understanding and Overcoming Negative Body Images," Eating Disorder Referral and Information Center, http://www.edreferral.com/body_image.htm (accessed October 13, 2008).

5. Christine Hartline, MA, "Dying to Fit In—Literally! Learning to Love Our Bodies and Ourselves," Eating Disorder Referral and Information Center, http://www.edreferral.com/body_image.htm (accessed October 13, 2008).

6. Gordon B. Forbes et al., "Body Dissatisfaction in Women and Men: The Role of Gender-Typing and Self-Esteem," *Sex Roles: A Journal of Research* (April 2001): http://findarticles.com/p/articles/mi_m2294/is_2001_April/ai_7 9856435?tag=content;col1, (accessed September 23, 2008).

7. Dondi Scumaci, "52 Ways to Build Your Child's Self-Esteem," online audio program published by *Sound Learning Solutions*, Rockhurst University Continuing Education Center, Inc., 2007.

8. Scumaci, *Designed for Success*.

## CHAPTER 6
## BREAK THE WORRY HABIT

1. Tracy, *The Psychology of Achievement*.

2. Dale Carnegie, *How to Stop Worrying and Start Living*, rev. ed. (New York: Pocket Books, 1990).

## CHAPTER 7
## BOUQUET OF THORNS

1. Don Colbert, MD, *Deadly Emotions* (Nashville, TN: Thomas Nelson Publishers, 2003).

2. Lewis B. Smedes, *Forgive and Forget: Healing the Hurts We Don't Deserve* (New York: HarperOne, 1996).

3. Ibid.

4. Story obtained from his appearance as guest speaker at Cornerstone Christian Church, San Antonio, Texas, April 27, 1997.

5. Dominic P. Herbt, "Restoring Relationships: Healing for the Brokenhearted," *Interactive Journal*, Sonrise House.

## CHAPTER 8
## TOXIC ALLIANCES

1. "Ethics and Integrity," a workshop by Dondi Scumaci.

2. Quoted from material prepared by The Center for Business and Ethics at Loyola Marymount University.

## CHAPTER 9
## EMBRACING CHANGE

1. William Bridges, *Managing Transitions: Making the Most of Change* (Cambridge, MA: Perseus Books, De Capo Press, 2003).

2. Doug Smart, compiler, *Thriving in the Midst of Change* (Roswell, GA: James & Brookfield Publishers, 2002).

3. Collins, *Good to Great*.

## CHAPTER 10
## BOLD BLESSINGS

1. George Bernard Shaw, *Pygmalion*, 4.135, viewed at http://www.bartleby.com/138/5.html (accessed October 13, 2008).

2. Adapted from a workshop developed by Dondi Scumaci titled, "Motivation, Morale, and Commitment: Designing Cultures that Breathe Success."

3. Diana Hagee, *Proclamations: Releasing the Power of God's Word* (San Antonio, TX: Global Evangelism Television, Inc., 2005).

## CHAPTER 11
## GRAND DESIGNS

1. Jim Loehr, *The Power of Story: Rewrite Your Destiny in Business and in Life* (New York: Free Press, 2007).

## CHAPTER 12
## MAKING IT REAL

1.    Adapted from a story submitted by Michele Borba, author unknown, in Jack Canfield and Mark Victor Hansen, *A 2nd Helping of Chicken Soup for the Soul* (Deerfield Beach, FL: HCI, 1994), 237–238.

## CHAPTER 13
## FIND YOUR BALANCE AND PROTECT YOUR PLAN

1.    Dr. Rick Brickman, "Life by Design: Making Lifestyle Choices That Contribute to Better Physical and Emotional Health," audio produced by *CareerTrack*.

## CHAPTER 14
## BROKEN FENCES AND OPEN GATES

1.    This section on boundaries is adapted from "Advice: Codependency and Boundaries," by Lynette Hoy, NCC, LCPC, National Certified Counselor, Licensed Clinical Professional Counselor, http://www.hoyweb.com/lh/codepend.htm (accessed October 15, 2008).

2.    Nancy Ellett Allison, PhD, "The Professional and Boundary Issues," *Christian Ethics Today*, February 1997.

## CHAPTER 15
## FRAMING LIFE EVENTS

1.    Wendy Edey, "What Would a Hopeful Person Do?" The Hope Foundation of Alberta, http://www.ualberta.ca/HOPE/literature/goodreading/Good%20Reading%20-%20What%20would%20a%20Hopeful%20person%20do.pdf (accessed November 11, 2008).

2.    Martin E. Seligman, *Learned Optimism: How to Change Your Mind and Your Life* (New York: Vintage, 2006).

3.    Gary S. Topchik, *Managing Workplace Negativity* (Saranac Lake, NY: AMACO, 2001).

4.    Ibid.

## CHAPTER 16
## GRACE AND GRATITUDE NOURISH HOPE

1.    Robert A. Emmons and Raymond F. Paloutzian, "The Psychology of Religion," *Annual Review of Psychology* 54 (2003): 377–402.

2.    Elizabeth Heubeck, MD, "Boost Your Health With a Dose of Gratitude," WebMD.com, http://women.webmd.com/guide/gratitute-health-boost (accessed October 15, 2008).

3.    Joan Borysenko, PhD, "Health and Balance: Practicing Gratitude," WebMD.com, http://www.webmd.com/balance/features/practicing-gratitude (accessed October 15, 2008).

4.    Tom Rath and Donald O. Clifton, research from *How Full Is Your Bucket? Positive Strategies for Work and Life*, http://www.bucketbook.com/content/default.aspx?ci=12301 (accessed October 15, 2008).

5.    Noelle C. Nelson, *The Power of Appreciation in Business: How an Obsession with Value Increases Performance, Productivity & Profits* (Esslingen, Germany: MindLab Publishing, 2005).

6.    Rath and Clifton, research from *How Full Is Your Bucket?*

7.    Nelson, *The Power of Appreciation in Business.*

8.    Dody Tsiantar, "The Cost of Incivility," *TIME*, February 7, 2005.

9.    This story was verbally given to me.

10.   Edey, "What Would a Hopeful Person Do?"

## CHAPTER 17
## REACH BEYOND YOUR COMFORT ZONE

1.    Tracy, *The Psychology of Achievement.*

2.    Sheila Wellington, *Be Your Own Mentor: Strategies from Top Women on the Secrets of Success* (New York: Random House, 2001).

3.    Marcus Buckingham and Donald Clifton, PhD, *Now, Discover Your Strengths* (New York: The Free Press, 2001), front flap.

## CHAPTER 18
## TRAINING THE VINE

1.    Adapted from *The Talent Management Handbook: Creating Organizational Excellence by Identifying, Developing, and Promoting Your Best People*, edited by Lance A. Berger and Dorothy R. Berger (New York: McGraw-Hill, 2004).

2.    John Maxwell, *Thinking for a Change: 11 Ways Highly Successful People Approach Life and Work* (New York: Warner Books, 2003).

3.    Harvey Mackay, *Dig Your Well Before You're Thirsty: The Only Networking Book You'll Ever Need* (New York: Doubleday Business, 1999).

4.    Andy Simmons, "How to Click and Clean," *Reader's Digest*, April 2008.

## CHAPTER 19
## LEARN FROM MASTER GARDENERS

1.    For more information about the topic of mentoring, go to www
.DondiScumaci.com.

## CHAPTER 20
## GROWING THROUGH ADVERSITY

1.    Adapted from Dutch Sheets, *Tell Your Heart to Beat Again: Discover the Good in What You're Going Through* (Ventura, CA: Gospel Light Publications, 2002).

2.    Earl Nightingale, *Essence of Success: 163 Lessons from the Dean of Self-Development* (Niles, IL: Nightingale-Conant, 1993).

3.    Mary Fahy, *The Tree That Survived the Winter*, illus. Emil Antonucci (Mahwah, NJ: Paulist Press, 2001).

## CHAPTER 21
## PULLING COMPLACENCY

1.    BrainyQuote.com, "Brian Tracy Quotes," http://www.brainyquote .com/quotes/quotes/b/briantracy386813.html (accessed October 17, 2008).

## CHAPTER 22
## KEEP ALL OF YOUR APPOINTMENTS WITH HOPE

1.    John Maxwell, *Encouragement Changes Everything* (Nashville, TN: Thomas Nelson, 2008).

# STEP UP, STEP OUT,
## ~ *and* ~
# BREAK THROUGH
## *at* WORK

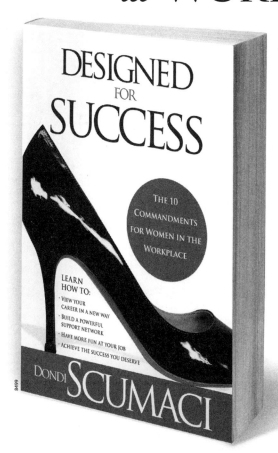

Women today face unique challenges and incredible opportunities in the workplace. In *Designed for Success*, Dondi Scumaci helps you take charge of your career and achieve the success and satisfaction you deserve.

Learn how to get ahead in today's workplace and make a difference to the organizations you serve and the lives you touch—without changing who you are.

978-1-59979-237-8
$21.99

## VISIT YOUR LOCAL BOOKSTORE.

EXcel
BOOKS
A STRANG COMPANY

Now that you've finished reading *Ready, Set...Grow!*, you are personally invited to visit www.dondiscumaci.com. Here you will find tools designed to help you get traction, build momentum, and make connections. It's as close as you can get to having Dondi as your personal mentor and so much more!

Stop by and check out the podcasts, newsletters, tips, and inspirations. Download book discussion guides, ask Dondi a question, and join the mentoring community.

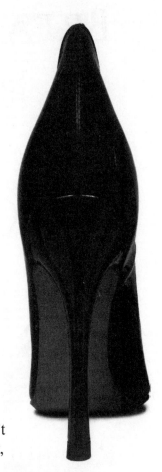

# dondi
## SCUMACI inc

Dondi travels extensively every year, leaving organizations around the world energized and ready to attain the next level of excellence.

If you are interested in having Dondi speak to your organization, please go to www.dondiscumaci.com for details on booking information and availability.

If you enjoyed *Ready Set...Grow!* and haven't read Dondi's first book, *Designed for Success*, pick up your copy today! *Designed* gives you the tools you need to take charge of your future, make a greater impact, and achieve the success you deserve.

# FREE NEWSLETTERS
## TO HELP EMPOWER YOUR LIFE

## Why subscribe today?

☐ **DELIVERED DIRECTLY TO YOU.** All you have to do is open your inbox and read.

☐ **EXCLUSIVE CONTENT.** We cover the news overlooked by the mainstream press.

☐ **STAY CURRENT.** Find the latest court rulings, revivals, and cultural trends.

☐ **UPDATE OTHERS.** Easy to forward to friends and family with the click of your mouse.

**CHOOSE THE E-NEWSLETTER THAT INTERESTS YOU MOST:**

- Christian news
- Daily devotionals
- Spiritual empowerment
- And much, much more

SIGN UP AT: **http://freenewsletters.charismamag.com**

8178